Real Estate Marketing on Facebook

Discover the Secrets of How a
Top Producing Team Used Facebook
to Help Drive Over $10 Million
in Annual Sales Volume

Chris Moore
John Cote

www.SocialMarketingTV.com

Real Estate Marketing on Facebook

Discover the Secrets of How a Top Producing Team
Used Facebook to Help Drive Over
$10 Million in Annual Sales Volume

Moore, Chris; Cote, John (2013-07-21)
Chris Moore Marketing LLC
Softcover, 1st Edition.

Warnings and Disclaimer

This book contains the opinions and research of its authors. The authors have successfully used many of the techniques described herein. This book was written with the intent to educate readers with helpful and informative information on the topics covered. It is sold with the understanding that the techniques and strategies covered in the book and associated materials may or may not be suitable for every business and are not guaranteed to produce any particular results.

The authors and publishers have made significant efforts to ensure the accuracy of the information provided and disclaim any responsibility for any liability, loss or risk, personal or otherwise, which is incurred as a consequence, directly or indirectly, from the use and application of any of the contents of this book and its associated materials.

Laws and practices often vary by state and country and readers are recommended to seek professional legal advice prior to application of any of the contents of this book and its associated materials.

The subtitle; <u>Discover the Secrets of How a Top Producing Team Used Facebook to Help Drive Over $10 Million in Annual Sales Volume</u>, refers to author Chris Moore, REALTOR®, and his business partner, Associate Broker Donna-Marie Chiroux's combined sales volume from June 2012 through May 2013. Sales volume is defined as the total closing prices of the homes sold during the stated period. Over 30% of their home sales were directly attributable to initial and follow up contacts made using Facebook.

There are multiple websites we have suggested as resources throughout this book. We do not profit in any way from recommending these sites. We have mentioned John's book, ***MOBILIZE YOUR CUSTOMERS*** several times as a resource. If you purchase his book, he receives a royalty for those sales of course.

About the Authors

Chris Moore is an anomaly. At least that is what his mother believes. A singularly focused individual, Chris launched his first business at the age of 8. Borrowing his father's PeachTree accounting software, Chris created a spreadsheet for his fledgling lawn business and hired his friends to help with the work. His parents laughed in awe when he made a point to set up specific line items for equipment maintenance and gas expenses. But it just seemed to make sense to his innately organized mind. And he hasn't stopped since. Chris Moore doesn't settle for mediocre. He dives into everything with 110%. That singular focus is matched by a seemingly bottomless well of enthusiasm, charisma, humor and energy.

Landing his first "real job" as busboy at the age of 12, Chris subsequently worked his way through the restaurant industry becoming a general manager at the age of 21. But, 70-hour workweeks do not a healthy family make, so in the summer of 2012, Chris joined his mother in the real estate business. Within six months, he tripled their sales and began referring clients to other agents. Chris Moore has a gift for marketing and generating business. His ability to see "holes" in the industry and reinvent the wheel are what inspired this book.

Chris is a devoted husband and father of two precious girls. He lives in Huntsville, Alabama and works full time as a licensed Realtor.

John Cote is the Award Winning Author of the Amazon.com #1 Best Selling Book, *MOBILIZE YOUR CUSTOMERS - Create Powerful Word of Mouth Advertising Using Social Media, Video and Mobile Marketing to Attract New Customers and Skyrocket Your Profits*. His company, Rocket Social Marketing, a certified member of the Power Marketing Consultants Network, creates growth strategies, marketing campaigns and lead capture systems for businesses and organizations of any size. The scientifically based systems they employ have been effectively used in over 350 industries globally to dramatically increase sales revenue.

A voracious reader, John invests a great deal of time researching the cutting edge trends in technology, social media and marketing. He is a frequent speaker and panelist on these topics as they relate to business innovation, increasing revenue and customer retention. His forthcoming book with co-author Ron J. Phillips will be published fall 2013 and is titled, ***ONWARDS! Master the Power of Accelerating Technological Change and Dominate Your Marketplace***.

John has a deep personal interest in emerging medical technologies since he has received surgically implanted stem cells to repair his injured knee, his wife is a two time cancer survivor and one of his sons has bilateral cochlear implants. He is an accomplished pilot having attained over 10,000 hours of flight time while serving in the U.S. Marine Corps and flying for a major U.S. airline. He and his wife Jennifer along with their daughter and two sons (plus 2 dogs) currently reside in Huntsville, Alabama.

Dedication

Chris

My thanks go out to my mother and my wife. These two women keep me going every day and always encourage me to strive for extreme levels of success. I would also like to thank my co-author, John Cote, for believing in me. Very rarely in life do I get the chance to meet someone who can easily stump me in a conversation and make me hungry to learn more and become better at what I do. Thank you for being that person.

John

I would like to thank my co-author Chris Moore, for his hard work, expertise and dedication in helping to make this project happen. I challenged him to step up to the plate and he did! Also, I want to thanks to my wife and children for their love and patience while I wrote another book.

Free Bonus

Thanks for buying the book. To get access to your free video interview with Chris and John "The Top 5 Mistakes Real Estate Professionals Make on Facebook and How To Fix Them!", scan your receipt from Amazon then email it to:

join-remarketingbook@instantcustomer.com

or scan the code:

Table of Contents

Introduction

Why should I use Facebook
to market my real estate business?

Facebook is an online social networking service. That is how Wikipedia defines the site, so it must be true. But that definition is far too simplistic for something so incredibly diverse and encompassing. If you were to ask a teenager, "What is Facebook?" You will surely get an answer similar to: "Facebook is a website where I can keep track of my friends and meet new people." Yes, Facebook is that too. Chris' favorite Facebook definition is, "Many things to many people." For him, this says it all. For many, this website is an escape from reality, to others a procrastination tool. For one of Chris' grandfathers, it is a tool to keep in touch with his extended family.

Now, let's ask some real estate agents and brokers, "What is Facebook?" Just for the sake of accuracy, Chris asked 10 people in his office and here were their responses.

"A distraction! A way to catch up with family." - Kyle

"Keep in touch with family and friends." - Tanya

"A way to connect; family, dating, personal, business. Connectability." - Michelle

"Facebook is a way to keep in touch with family and to promote my business." - Kat

"Social connection." - Kayla

"Waste of time." - Daniel

"A bad source of gossip." - Charles

"A way to contact old classmates and past friends." - Anne

"A path to connection with others in the moment that they are in their moments." - Rob

"Way for people to connect. I think it's a waste of time." - Laura

Wow! Only two people even mentioned their business. This doesn't surprise us one bit simply because most agents that we have met don't know where to start. Here are the most common complaints Chris hears in the office:

- I have my Facebook Business page set up and I don't know what to do with it now.

- How did you get your page to look so professional? Why can't I do that?

- I don't have many likes on my page.

- I don't know what to post. What should I post?

- I've been active on my Business page for months and I haven't gotten one referral or lead! What am I doing wrong?

The reason we are writing this book is to answer these questions. But the big question for many agents is: "Why should I use Facebook to market my business?"

What if we told you that we knew of a way to market your business to a controlled demographic and a selected audience using branded advertising. How about the ability to drive traffic to your website, increase your referral business, keep in constant contact with your past clients, and farm for new listings and buyers FOR FREE. How about it you could do it in less than 30 minutes per week?

Sign me up! Right? Chances are that you are already signed up and so are your prospective and past clients. According to Quora.com, a popular question and answer website, 41.6% of Americans are active Facebook users. Let's break that down a bit... 41.6% of Americans over the age of 13? No. 41.6% of the ENTIRE United States population are active Facebook users. Can you think of any other marketing medium or advertising strategy to reach a larger audience for free than this?

The reason we wrote this book was simple. Chris has been very successful using Facebook to generate leads that turn into closings. He frequently has agents approach him and ask for tips on how he does it. Inevitably, every time he does, there will be several to a dozen agents listening in and taking notes! We decided it was time to get this information out in an organized, easy to follow book that teaches exactly how he does it.

After analyzing the results from Chris' team lead tracker starting in January 2013, he came to the conclusion that roughly 35% of their leads came from Facebook. That may not sound like a lot, but they consistently produce over 50 new leads per month overall. Those are very impressive numbers that most agents would do almost anything for. So 35% of 50 equals 17 leads on average per month. Leads don't put food on the table or pay the mortgage of course, and not all or even most of these leads turned into closings or active buyers or sellers. Every month, 3 to 4 of these leads head to the closing table within 60 days. That's a minimum 17% conversion rate from Facebook to the closing table. This year Chris' average commission has been $4,200, times 3 to 4 transactions per month; you do the math.

Chris' father once told him the famous quote, "Sales is a numbers game" and he was he right in many respects. Most of you have already figured out selling or leasing real estate is no exception. Increase your number of leads and you will most likely increase your revenue.

Fan page to Business page

What is the difference between a Facebook Fan page and a Facebook Business page? A Facebook Business page represents a business; it is indeed also a Fan page for that business. Classifying a page as a Fan page is more appropriate when you are creating a page for a cause you are supporting, artist, band or public figure, or a non-profit organization. Fan pages aren't necessarily for selling products of services to businesses or consumers, while Business pages are. So to sum it up, Business pages are Fan pages. But Fan pages do not have to be for a business.

Statistics that might surprise you

According to the National Association of REALTORS® (NAR) Monthly Membership report, statistics show that there are 997,148 members as of May 30, 2013 and 1,377 local associations. That is a lot of REALTORS®!

Did you know that 90% of homebuyers look on the Internet, 87% use a real estate agent, and 53% use a yard sign according to the 2012 NAR Profile of Home Buyers and Sellers? So only 10% of homebuyers are not looking on the Internet. Are these 10% the people you are targeting in your marketing? If they are, good luck to you. In our experience, real estate can be a numbers game and Chris designs his marketing plans with that in mind.

The 2012 REALTOR® Technology Survey states that 89% of REALTORS® use social media to some extent. The vast majority of them are not using social media to market themselves or their businesses. Chances are those who do are doing it incorrectly. Read this book then implement what we teach and you will not be one of them.

The 4 Golden Rules of Marketing on Facebook

You will notice that we refer to these rules several times throughout this book for a reason. They are vital to promoting your business in a positive way. Facebook is a public forum and you have to assume that your posts are permanent. So, when posting on Facebook, make sure your posts comply with the 4 Golden Rules.

1. ALWAYS be positive and appropriate.

2. Ask yourself, does this post generate positive Facebook conversation?

3. Does this post promote my business, my company and/or my market in a positive light?

4. When in doubt... DON'T!

Constant Change

Almost everything in our world today is constantly evolving and changing, often too quickly for us to keep up. One of Chris' favorite commercials of all time displays constant change well. One by one the camera shows someone working on a laptop and captures each person's reaction when they see an advertisement for the "latest technology" machine. His favorite actress in this commercial yells out, "But I just bought this one!" The message we are trying to convey here is that Facebook is no different. Facebook has teams in place whose sole purpose is to constantly improve their systems and the user experience. They make several large changes every year in their quest for improvement and progression.

Periodically, we will release new editions of this book to keep you updated with any major changes that will affect you and the way you market your business on Facebook. Even better, we encourage you to Like us and follow the conversation at Facebook.com/RealEstateMarketingBook to learn more about new cutting edge approaches to earn business on Facebook and other social media sites.

Facebook must be a priority

How important is brushing your teeth in the morning? Important enough that you make it a priority to do so daily. You should approach the time spent on your Facebook Business account with this same attitude and repetition. You may be thinking to yourself, "Facebook is huge! There is an abundance of opportunities." You're right. But we challenge you to think like this: "Facebook is huge! There is an abundance of missed opportunities." Don't miss the opportunities. If you don't make Facebook a priority, your competitors will and they will be selling houses. You may be the one who is still struggling to get by. There are 1 billion people using Facebook. You just need to connect with a few hundred to a thousand in your community to get your piece of the pie.

There is massive opportunity to win the business of buyers and sellers online. You just need to master the approach. Gary Keller, founder of Keller Williams Realty and author of THE MILLIONAIRE REAL ESTATE AGENT, has a ton of fantastic tips and advice in his book. To us, the most important quote and takeaway is this, "You can never have enough good leads." We wholeheartedly agree. Although this is obvious, many of you don't. Every successful agent has a constant stream of leads coming into their business. This book will teach you the techniques you need to keep YOUR funnel of leads full.

To ensure this book is an easy read, the rest will be written with Chris' voice, however the concepts and techniques come from both authors. We are excited and honored to share our Facebook strategies and secrets with you in this book and we wish you prosperity and success in your business!

Chapter 1

How can I benefit from having a Facebook business page?

An agent in my office once asked me to help her set up her Facebook Business page and I replied with, "Why?" You guessed it; this stopped her in her tracks and she was even taken back a bit. The expected answers were: "Sure", or "Yes, but it will have to be later on this afternoon", or maybe even, "No." But I guarantee she wasn't prepared for my response. Her answer was highly predictable, "Because I don't know how to do it." That's an honest answer, but did she really answer my question?

Why? It's such a powerful question! This simple three-letter word can be used in so many ways; people interpret the word's meaning or implications differently almost every time this question is asked. What I was really wondering with my question to her was why she wants to set up a Facebook Business page. As we went deeper into the conversation, I continued to break down her answer and repeated my original question until we finally came to this conclusion, "Someone told me that I need a Facebook Business page as a real estate professional."

So often in this business we assume that something is a necessity just because everyone else is doing it. We are so busy trying to stay current with technology and ahead of our competitors, that we lose sight of the 'Why?' So change your 'Why?' from because someone told you that you needed a Facebook Business page to I will use Facebook to market my business effectively and to actively generate leads and quality referrals.

How can I benefit from having a Facebook business page?

The phrase "let me count the ways" come to mind when I read this question. There are SO many benefits to having a good

Facebook Business page, if you implement it correctly and stay persistent. Here is a list of benefits that should be near the top of your list:

- Easily keep in touch with past clients.

- Market your listings to a targeted group of people and income demographic.

- Farm for future and now buyers.

- The ability to educate your audience on trends in your local housing market, establishing yourself as an expert.

- Be the source! Share current events and news stories as well as original blogs that directly or indirectly pertain to the real estate market in your area.

- REMIND PEOPLE THAT YOU SELL REAL ESTATE!

Easily keep in touch with past clients

Before we started this book, I asked my mother (who is my business partner and in the top 1% of agents in our area for sales) what Facebook means to her. This was her response: "Facebook is the very best way I know to keep in touch with my past clients without being too intrusive. To subtly and consistently remind them that I am a working REALTOR®." Great answer, Mom! A "like" here or a small comment there can keep you in the mind of your past clients. It lets them know that you are paying attention and you are interested in their lives and how they are doing. And it doesn't take a lot of time – maybe 10 minutes a day. My mother has been doing this for years and it obviously works.

Pay Attention

Keep in mind that, in most cases, people post things that are important to them. These comments create a perfect opportunity to remind them that THEY are important to you. If you see that one of your clients is getting married, make a comment – a simple 'Congratulations!!' will do. Or 'like' the photo of their two year old spreading peanut butter all over the kitchen counter. If it was important enough for them to post it, it's important enough for you to notice!

I particularly love when they post home improvement projects. This is a perfect opportunity for you to compliment them with something like "Wow! Way to amp up your resale value, Joe! Makes your REALTOR® very happy!" That one simple comment accomplishes three very important things.

1. You are publicly edifying Joe in front of all his friends.

2. You are reminding everyone that you helped Joe find & buy that house.

3. You are letting all of Joe's friends know you are his real estate agent thereby exposing your business to people who you haven't met (yet).

Market your listings to a targeted group of people and income demographics

A question agents and brokers commonly hear from sellers is, "In what ways, and how will you market my home if I list it with you?" Let's be honest... How many of you refer to Facebook as a primary medium to market your listings? If you do, that's great, but it is working?

Marketing your listings on Facebook can be done in many different ways, but the main objective is to reach the largest audience possible and more particularly people who may be in the market to buy and who can afford it! We will get into building an audience that can produce results later in the book.

What is tagging?

Facebook describes tagging as, "A tag is a special kind of link. When you tag someone, you create a link to their timeline." You may be thinking, how does tagging photos tie in with my Business page? Automatic participation. Tagging your clients and other friends will make them feel included and likely lead them to engage in conversations on your page!

Please note: **Facebook does not allow Business or Fan pages to tag individuals in photos or posts, only other Business or Fan pages.** To tag individuals on a post or photo posted by a Business page, you must do so from a personal account.

For example, you want to post a photo of a home you just sold and you were the buyer's agent. Post the photo on your Business page and then switch to Use Facebook As your PERSONAL account. Next, visit your Business page as a consumer. Now you have the option to tag individuals on the picture. This is a bit of an inconvenience, but maybe Facebook will change their policies regarding this matter one day in the future.

Tag your sellers! When you are posting photos and info about your listings on Facebook, always, always, always, always tag your sellers. Was that subtle enough? This one quick step automatically makes that post visible to all your seller's friends, thereby exponentially increasing your audience. As an added bonus, it exposes you and your business AGAIN to people you don't know (aka potential clients.)

Please note: **You can only tag individuals who are on your friends list. Make it a point to become friends with all of your clients, buyers and sellers.** This has to be a priority to help market their home or property. Not all of your clients will want to do this and that's fine but you should definitely try. Also, be sure to encourage your clients to 'Like' your Business page. I will go over this in greater detail later in the book.

Follow this same procedure when you sell a house. Post a photo of the home, congratulate your buyers on their purchase and then tag your buyer in the post. What does this accomplish? It makes the buyer feel wonderful and by tagging them in the post, it allows all of their friends to see their new home and exposes you as their real estate agent to a wider audience of folks you have yet to meet. Be sure to ask and receive permission to do so, some people are more private and will not oblige.

Are you seeing a pattern here? What is the main objective for using Facebook to promote your business? Acquiring positive exposure and the opportunity to increase your sphere of influence.

How do I tag people in photos?

Remember, tagging people in photos and posts can only be done while Using Facebook As your PERSONAL account.

Tag photos

Step 1: Locate the photo on your Business page, click on the photo.

Step 2: Directly below the photo there, you may see up to six options to choose from. Click on the Tag Photo option, which should be the first one listed.

Step 3: Click on the person in the photo and you will be prompted to find which one of your friends is represented. Type in the person's name until it appears then click on the appropriate result.

You have now tagged someone in the photo. When you are finished tagging, simply press the Done Tagging option below the picture.

HINT: *Tagging someone in a photo doesn't mean they have to be present in the picture. It's OK to tag people in a photo of a house or beautiful scenery.*

Tag people in posts

Step 1: Locate the post on your Business page

Step 2: Click comment, and leave a comment on the post. At the end of your comment, type: "with (the name of the person(s) you would like to tag in the post.)" Be sure to click on their name when it shows up. This is a pivotal step in the process of tagging. If you misspell their name, they will not show up in the results.

Tagging in posts works beautifully. This will notify whoever was tagged in the post and they will now be engaged in the conversation and will likely be visiting your Business page.

Farm for *future buyers* and *now buyers*

Farming for buyers may be one of the easiest and most rewarding tasks you can do using Facebook to grow your business. This is where your website comes into play, (if your website allows consumers to search for homes), but can be achieved by agents who do not have a website as well. One of the best ways to attract buyers is to share links embedded into posts and status updates that will take your audience directly to a specific home search results page on your website. The page should display a list of homes for sale in an affordable price range and more importantly in desirable locations and neighborhoods. Any lead from your website should drop right into your email inbox.

Watch for trends in your market. For instance, if the market is trending toward 4 bedroom homes under 200,000 in the newer school district south of town, create a search specifically displaying homes that meet those criteria. Once the buyers start searching on your site, they are truly captured. Now that they are in a controlled environment, all leads automatically lead to you!

What if I don't have a website? It's okay; there are other ways to farm for buyers on Facebook. One way is to offer your audience a current list of homes for sale. Sounds easy enough, right? But how do you get people to opt in to receive this list? Here's an idea; every so often post a poll or questionnaire. People love to give their opinions! Try something like this:

"Questionnaire! I am conducting some market research to see what new homebuyer's have on their 'Must Have' list and which are the most desirable neighborhoods in our city. I'd REALLY appreciate your feedback; please be realistic.

What is on your 'Must Have' list?

Is there a neighborhood or community that you can see yourself as a part of in the future?

More and more buyers are looking for homes with a Mother-in-law suite, could this be a necessity in your future?

Thank you for your participation. The Questionnaire will be open for 1 week, ending on May 13th. I will post the results on May 14th! The Top 10 Must-Haves and Top 5 Neighborhoods. Be sure to check back to see how your answers match up."

Post this twice a day for the duration of the questionnaire. It would be unrealistic to believe that posting this one time will give the appropriate exposure necessary to get adequate participation. If you have a large number of followers on your Fan page, you may be able to ask once.

Using online surveys embedded in Facebook

There are plenty of different applications available for free or a small fee on Facebook for creating very easy-to-use surveys that will increase the engagement of current and potential clients on your page. Facebook's own simple survey is a great place to start since it's very easy-to-use. There are not a lot of options but it works very well and gets the job done. Just type in a search for "Facebook survey app" and you will come up with plenty of different applications available like Survey Monkey, Snap App and many others. Just like any other application that you install on your Facebook fan page, they are easy to use and implement.

Encouraging audience participation is always a great idea. Also, be sure to post the results. This again will attract plenty of attention from your audience and by inviting them back to see the results, you will keep them engaged and interested in visiting your page. The surveys can be on current events (locally or nationally), style and design questions regarding remodeling projects like kitchens and bathrooms, should the local school board build a new school at a particular location, who will win American Idol or Dancing With the

Stars, etc. The questions don't always have to be real estate related, but some should be.

How does this poll help me farm for buyers? Take each person's answers and conduct a search on your MLS and send them the results. Chances are, one of the participants will be encouraged by your findings and become engaged as an active buyer. You'll never know if you don't try. So give it a shot!

The ability to educate your audience on trends in your local housing market, thus establishing yourself as an expert.

Chances are, the majority of your Facebook friends are local. As we touched on in the previous section, you can create specific searches and blogs to educate your friends on what's happening in the market. A lot of real estate agents and brokers make the mistake of thinking that the general public is interested in market stats or industry related blogs. The reality is, most buyers or potential buyers don't care about stats and they certainly don't want to strain their brains trying to decipher graphs and market trends. These folks want to know how market trends affect THEM specifically – and preferably in 300 words or less. Which brings us to our next point... the key to effective Blogging on Facebook.

Keep your blogs current and viable

Watch what's happening in the market. Pay attention to which television shows are popular on the home improvement channels. Check out the latest issue of home, gardening and design magazines. What are they talking about on the cover? Those television stations & magazine publishers pay big money hiring the very best marketing firms to watch for trends in the market. What are people talking about? What's hot? For instance, we once wrote a blog post about the hottest paint color trends for the year simply because my mom was obsessing over what color to paint her new home. That one blog post generated more generic hits on Facebook and our website than any we had ever written. Why? Well, honestly it was a happy accident. By chance, we happened to post it in March when folks were beginning to think about getting their homes ready to sell. But, this taught us the importance of staying current.

Be the source! Share current events and news that directly or indirectly pertain to the real estate market

Again, pay attention to what's happening in your market and how it affects housing trends. School zoning is obviously a huge driver when it comes to real estate. School closings & restructuring, test scores, and awards, particularly those that generate national attention can alter public perception and real estate markets pretty quickly. Parks and public facilities can also have a positive effect on real estate markets. Keep yourself informed and you'll never lack for something exciting and POSITIVE to write about. Remember our Golden Rules? STAY positive. Never use your Facebook Business page or website as a forum to complain. Would a good sales person speak negatively about his/her product? Always remember that your real estate market is your product.

An example of a post I made on my Business page a few months ago is perfect for what I am talking about. Huntsville, the city where I live and sell real estate, was in the running with 11 other cities nationwide to host the 2013 Social Media Tourism Symposium. Huntsville had no problem rising to the top and, one by one, beating out the competition. This is HUGE for Huntsville, AL! I shared a link to the Symposium's Facebook Fan Page and a link to an article in the local paper telling people more about the competition. Remember, be the source!

This is the type of thing you want to share with your audience on Facebook. Positive, uplifting events or news that is relevant to your city and communities you serve.

REMIND PEOPLE THAT YOU SELL REAL ESTATE!

This can be a little tricky – a little goes a long way. There is a fine line between reminding folks that you are a real estate practitioner and shoving it down their throats. Remember, that Facebook users have the option to 'HIDE' news feeds from friends that annoy them. If you flood your personal Facebook page with links to your listings or other real estate-oriented posts, chances are good you'll get the boot. I hide friends who are agents all the time and I'm in the business.

One of the best ways I've found to remind folks that I sell houses is to post short little messages about meeting cool new clients or how much I love showing houses on a sunny Sunday afternoon. Keep it short, sweet and again... always positive.

Importance of linking your personal and business page

I have consulted with dozens of real estate agents regarding their Internet marketing campaigns, especially Facebook Business pages. The biggest obstacle that I continuously come across is during my initial look at what the agent has already set up on their page. Notice, I didn't say Business page... About 50% of the time, when I look to see which stage of the set up routine an agent is in, I find that they have created another personal page to represent their real estate business. This is a good thing to catch early when I am consulting because it gives me an excuse to start over and implement what I teach.

This, of course, is against Facebook's Terms of Service (TOS.) You are only allowed one personal profile and businesses are not allowed to create personal profiles. That's what Fan pages are for.

This is very important. When signing up to join Facebook you must start by creating a personal account. To create a Fan or Business page, you must be already logged in and Using Facebook As your personal account. So, how is it that some agent's personal and Business pages aren't linked? This brings us to another interesting situation I run into sporadically: I find that an agent has created a second personal account to use to create their Business page. I can see how this could make sense to some people, considering their intentions of maintaining separation between their business and personal accounts. This is actually counterproductive and it's against the Facebook TOS.

Here's another statistic for you, about 70% of agents that I've come across find Facebook to be quite overwhelming. Does this sound familiar? Odd as it sounds, many agents feel obligated to create a Facebook Business page (known to many as a "Fan page") because everyone else is doing it. This takes me back to my childhood and the ideology behind peer pressure and standard expectations set by society. And it brings up a question, "Why would you want to do what everyone else is doing? How does that set you and your Business apart from your competitors?" For example, every agent in my office has a website for their business. I am not saying don't create a website because everyone else has one and you should be different. My point is to make your website different. Highlight what makes your business unique and SHOUT IT FROM THE ROOF TOPS! This is what captures the attention of your audience and prospective clients if you allow it. It's what makes you different and can be what defines you and your business.

Creating your Facebook Business page while logged into your personal page makes it so much easier to invite your friends and circle of influence to 'Like' your page. If you already have your Business page established with a ton of 'Likes', I am not telling you to delete it! Don't worry, there is a way to link your existing Business page and your personal page together and we will go over that in the next chapter.

Linking your accounts together serves other purposes as well:

- Allows you switch back and forth from your business to personal accounts with the click of a button

- Only one username and password to remember

- It will be much easier to share your Business page posts with people on the friend list of your personal page.

Facebook auto populates your list of friends from your personal page into your business page to give you an opportunity to invite each and every one of them.

Is linking your personal and Business page together absolutely essential? No, but why wouldn't you? In order to implement the strategies we teach in this book, it's essential. Also, keep in mind that real estate is a very personal business. Your clients are inviting you into their homes and financial lives in a very personal way. Linking your business and personal pages allows the clients to easily get a glimpse into your life and helps strengthen that bond. Some agents and brokers feel that remaining aloof reinforces their image as the professional real estate authority. That works for some people, but I totally disagree. It is possible to be completely professional and human at the same time. The more human and personal you can be with your clients, the easier it is to build trust and solid lasting relationships. Solid, lasting relationships lead to building advocates for you business – you'll learn more about advocates later in the book.

Posting Business on Personal

You've just learned more about how important it is to link your Business pages and personal pages together, and there is one more thing to pay close attention to! **Posting business related posts on your personal page is frowned upon.** If this weren't a big issue, Fan and Business pages would have never been created! With that being said, it's common for people to do this anyway. If this is you, be very careful. I am in no way giving you permission or telling you it's okay to intermingle business and pleasure on Facebook, but I do advise you to keep specific business posts under 10% of your personal posts. Best-selling authors and Facebook experts Mari Smith and Amy Porterfield also recommend 10% as a reasonable percentage as well.

Keep it clean!

Remember our Golden Rules! Facebook is a very public forum. We want our clients and friends to see us as human beings, but also respect us as professional business people. So, watch what you post on your personal page. Sharing posts with profanity, inappropriate content or rabid political sentiments can give the wrong impression and may ultimately hurt your business. Even if your personal and business pages are not linked, clients may still have access to your personal page, so keep it clean and positive. And remember our fourth Golden Rule – When in doubt... DON'T. If you are questioning whether or not it's a good idea, it probably isn't.

Chapter 2

Creating and customizing your Facebook business page.

One of the best things about Facebook is that it is FREE! Sure there are certain things you can do to pay Facebook money if you want to, but it is truly optional. Maybe one day you will find it necessary to "Promote" your posts and statuses to reach an even broader audience, but this is not a necessity for most agents.

In the last chapter I went into detail about the importance of linking your personal and business pages together; so now let's implement.

What if I already have a Facebook Business page?

If you already have an established Facebook Business page with quite an audience, you are welcome to skip to the end of this chapter where I will show you step by step how to link your personal and existing accounts. **However, I highly recommend you read through the step-by-step instructions below regardless.** One small error or miscategorization can and does make a huge difference. Here are the top three mistakes people make when setting up a Fan or Business page:

1. **Miscategorizing your business type**. Recently Facebook has enhanced the Fan and Business page setup process. New business categories are available to choose from! If your existing Business page has been set up prior to January 2013, go back and ensure your page is categorized correctly.

2. **Creating a business page as a personal account**. We have already mentioned that this is in direct violation of Facebook's terms and use. If this is what you have done, start

over. The step-by-step instructions are listed next to properly create a Business page.

3. **Incomplete profile.** Like I mentioned, Facebook has recently enhanced the set up process for Fan and Business pages. More input fields are now available for pertinent information that helps your audience learn more about you and your business. This information is labeled Public Info, to edit this information locate the Admin Panel above your cover photo on your Business profile page. On the top right side select the drop down icon named Edit Page. The first option on the drop down list is Update Public Info. Review what you have previously included in this section and fill any blank fields with the appropriate information.

Creating a Facebook Business page

Step 1: Log in to your personal Facebook account and make sure you are on your home page.

HINT: *You will reach your home page by clicking the Facebook logo in the top left corner as long as you are logged into your account.*

Step 2: On the left side of the page under your name the Facebook logo you will find a few categories. Move your cursor over the PAGES header until you see MORE. Click on MORE.

Step 3: Near the top of the page you will find an option to + Create a Page. Click the button to take you to the next step.

Step 4: As a Real Estate agent, you want to pick the option: Local Business or Place. Working with buyers, sellers, landlords, and renters is a business.

Step 5: Fill out the following fields to correctly represent your business.

HINT: *Don't forget to check the "I agree to Facebook Pages Terms" radio button.*

Then click "Get Started".

Now you have a Facebook Business Page! But, there are many things left to do to customize your page to your specifications.

Customize your Facebook Business page

Step 6: Customize! There are many fields and spaces now that are ready for you to enter your specific information. Let's start near the top above your Page Name, click on + **Add Profile Picture.** Follow the prompt to choose a picture from file to use as your profile picture.

HINT: *After adding the profile picture, if you are not satisfied with the margins or appearance of the photo, press the **Edit Profile Picture** button and choose the **Edit Thumbnail** option. This will allow you to select **Scale to Fit**, which should improve the placement of your picture. ALSO, using a small file size picture will help tremendously achieve the look you are going for*

Step 7: To the right of the profile picture you will see an option to **Add a Cover**. The cover photo should be unique and express the purpose of what your page is about.

If you are reading this book, chances are we know what the purpose of your business is. Let's dig deeper than that. What is UNIQUE about your business? Do you specialize in staging? Are you a Certified Short Sale and Foreclosure Resource? Do you focus on relocation or luxury homes? Are you a Buyer's Agent? What makes you different from every other agent in your market or on Facebook, and why should consumers even consider you? Once you have answered these questions, represent your specialty in this cover photo.

On my team's business page I use the header from my website, TourHuntsville.com as my cover photo most often. You see, this is what makes my business UNIQUE in my local market. Not many agents or real estate companies can provide consumers with a resource quite like it. So that is what I advertise and highlight in my cover photo. You can learn how to create your own resource like TourHuntsville.com in our advanced training.

Step 8: Now, below your profile picture there are a few lines of information that you must edit and add information. Start by clicking on the first line, **Choose a Category**. Here you will want to type "Real Estate Agent, Real Estate Firm, Property Manager", or whatever is applicable. This will once again help your audience to associate your page with Real Estate.

Displayed in the second and third lines should be your address and phone number(s). These should have auto-populated from the information you have provided back in **Step 5**.

Lastly, at the bottom of the four lines, click on **Add Your Hours**.

HINT: *Unless YOU specifically have walk-in hours at your office in which you are the agent on duty, I recommend choosing Always Open. We all know that a real estate professional's job is never done, and most of us don't know what a day off feels like.*

Step 9: Finally! The last step in the initial customization of your Facebook Business page is to appropriately fill in the **About** section. You will find the **About** button directly below the Hours of Operation field that you just edited.

Click **About**, and this will take you to a new page. Here you will find a section labeled **Basic Info**. At the top right hand corner, look for the **Edit** button.

Once again, you will be rerouted to a new page. One by one, fill in the appropriate information. You will need to fill in the follow fields: Username, Start Date, Start Type, Short Description, Description, Email and Website.

HINT: *You may be wondering why you skipped the Official Page option. This category is applicable if your page is an unofficial page representing a brand, celebrity or organization. Since you are creating this Facebook Business page to market YOUR business, this will not apply to you.*

Username: You can customize your Page web address by selecting a unique Username. It will appear in the location bar of your browser after "https://www.facebook.com/" when you view your Page for example: https://www.facebook.com/tourhuntsville.

Go to http://www.facebook.com/username to set your custom domain name.

Note: *You will need to get a minimum of 25 likes before you can change this, make sure you are positive about the name. Once you name it and get to 100 likes, it cannot be changed.*

Start Date: Here you will simply add the year in which you began working in Real Estate.

Start Type: In this section you may choose from several options. Whatever you pick will be directly related to your start date so choose appropriately. The options given are: Born, Founded, Started, Opened, Created, and Launched.

Above, if you typed 2010 as your **Start Date** and that is when you first began to work as a licensed real estate professional, then you would select Started. Another situation might be that you opened your own firm in 2005 and the Facebook Business page is representing your company. Then the appropriate selection would be Founded, Opened, Created, or Launched.

Short Description and Description: This is where you announce to your audience what you do! In the **Short Description** you might write "Specialize in assisting sellers to sell their home using staging and increasing the curb appeal of their home." In the **Description** section, simply elaborate and add more information about you and what makes you UNIQUE within your local marketplace.

Lastly, **Email** and **Website**: Enter the email address that you wish for people to use to contact you. Then provide the web address of your website.

HINT: *If you do not have a website, or you are not yet comfortable with the site you have, list a web address for your company.*

Linking your existing Facebook Business page and personal account

Step 1: Log in to your *personal* account.

Step 2: Locate the search bar at the top of the page. This area will be available no matter which page you are on, including your profile page or news feed. In the search bar, type in the name of your Facebook Business page. If you have already 'Liked' your Business page, it should be the first option in the results. If not, your Business page might show up a little further down on the result lists. Click to go to your Business page.

Step 3: If you have yet to 'Like' this page, do so now. Then log out of your *personal* account.

Step 4: Log into your Business account and go to your profile page.

HINT: *Ever find yourself lost and trying to find your profile page? At any given time you can get back to your profile page with one click. At the top of the page to the right you will find a thumbnail of your profile picture along with your Business page's name. Click that icon; this will take you directly to your profile page every time. This trick also works while logged into your personal account.*

Step 5: On the bottom left side of the Admin Panel above your cover and profile picture is a small section named **Get More Likes**. Due east of the title you will see an option to **See Likes**, click this button.

Step 6: A pop-up window will appear with a list of all the people who 'Like' your page. Locate your *personal* profile and click the **Make Admin** button to the right.

Be sure that Manager is selected. This will allow you to do anything you need or want to do regarding your business page.

Becoming an administrator of your Business page will alleviate the need to log in using your Business page username and password. You now have the ability to login to your personal account and possess the ability to switch back and forth between accounts.

Important Safety Tip!

We highly recommend you have at least one other person that you trust as an administrator of your Fan page. If for any reason you lose your personal Facebook page, you will still have access to your Business page. If you are the only administrator and you lose your account, you just lost access to your page. If you have an employee or assistant as an admin and they quit, you need to immediately remove their admin privileges.

There are more detailed instructions in Chapter 6, but this will get you started. To add someone as an admin they need to be your friend and it's easier if they like the page. Get logged onto your Fan page profile, then you can look them up under your "likes." There is a button next to their profile picture you can click to "add as admin." You can also go to the admin panel on your fan page and click the *edit page* drop down menu, then click *manage admin roles*. That will take you to a page where you can start typing the new admin's name or email address. Facebook will auto-populate that field with their profile and you can select it to verify them. You have the ability to select what level of access they have from *manager, content creator, moderator, advertiser* and *insights analyst*. The new administrator will get a Facebook message notifying them that they are now a page admin.

Switching back and forth is easy

To navigate from one account to the other is as easy as clicking a button. Locate the gear icon on the top right corner of the page. Click this icon. A drop down menu will appear and you will see *Use Facebook as*: following one or more profile names and thumbnail pictures. If you are using Facebook as your personal profile, you will now see your Business page, and vice versa.

Get going!

Now you are off and running, the next step is adding content, photos, videos, and customizing your Facebook Business page to properly represent your business.

Chapter 3

Adding quality content, photos, and videos.

Content is a multifaceted word but the definition that is pertinent to the topic at hand as defined by thefreedictionary.com is this. *The material, including text and images, that constitutes a publication or document.* Another way of thinking about this is using the word substance i.e., the meat and potatoes of your Facebook Business page. This sounds like a daunting task, over-whelming perhaps, but it doesn't have to be. Many times, you, a real estate agent or broker, already possess the materials and knowledge to create massive amounts of content! The realization that what you do on a daily basis can easily be transformed into the meat and potatoes of your Facebook page is the first step.

Think about it... what do you do every day? Some daily real estate tasks for many of you may be previewing homes, putting a home on the market, going to lunch with a friend or client, searching through the MLS, or going to a closing (optimistically.) But how can I use these activities to add content to my Facebook Business page? It's actually quite simple. Let's use the examples above and go through them one by one.

Previewing houses – I am in no way telling you to take pictures of the homes you were previewing and advertising them on Facebook. Do not post other agent's listings on Facebook without permission! Remember the fourth Golden Rule, when in doubt... don't.

But what you can do is document your thoughts like a journal. For example, you could create a post similar to this: "Spent the day previewing 3 bedroom homes in South Nashville. So many cool retro homes on the market right now! Wish I could find one with 4 bedrooms!" What does this accomplish? 1) First and foremost, it reminds folks (again) that you are in real estate. 2) If one of your Facebook friends is into retro homes, it may inspire them to think about buying. 3) If one of your Facebook friends has a 4 bedroom retro house in South Nashville, maybe it will inspire them to sell and list it with you!

Let me share a story with you. It comes back to our Golden Rule of always staying positive when posting on Facebook. As agents, we often see some 'interesting' homes. Let's face it – sometimes the seller's décor choices can be downright scary. I once heard about an agent that routinely posted photos of what she called the 'Tackiest Homes of the Month' using MLS photos from homes in her own market. These were not her listings, simply homes she had seen while out showing and/or previewing homes. BAD idea! Not only did she offend the sellers, but the listing agents and sellers of these homes went ballistic. I'd imagine that she was simply trying to be funny and probably meant no harm, but Facebook is a public forum. To say it came back to bite her was an understatement.

Putting a home on the market – This one sounds too obvious! All I have to do is post the picture on my Business page and create a post with the picture, how many beds, baths, price and square footage, right? Yes, that's a good start, but that's a one-time thing. The post goes up, and then it's in the past. It doesn't just disappear, but it will not be at the forefront of your audience's mind when they visit your page. So, let's dig a little deeper. There are several other ways to use your listings to create good relevant content. Here are a few ideas:

- Every time you get a new listing, change your cover photo to a picture of your new listing - HINT: *Your cover photo is the large backdrop behind your profile picture at the top of your Facebook business page.*

- Wouldn't that make your seller happy?

- If listings are a huge part of your business, this can become one of your favorite weapons in the arsenal of marketing techniques.

- Make sure you alert your sellers that they are the "Home of the Week" on your Facebook Business page and you are featuring them exclusively for that time period.

- Tag your sellers in the photo and post of your new listing. This will give them a sense of ownership not just to the home, but to the marketing of their home. I know this won't work for every seller, but for sellers that are on Facebook, this can give you HUGE bonus points.

- When the seller is tagged, all of their Facebook friends see it. This gives you the opportunity to recruit for new 'Likes' through your sellers circle of influence and friends list, as well as new buyer and seller leads.

- Encourage your sellers to share the posts and announce to the world that their home is for sale! Once again, what great exposure for your listing!

- Team up with your mortgage lender of choice and ask them to provide you with financing information, special programs they might be running, and estimated monthly payments for the home you are featuring. Then in turn, create another post displaying the quotes and information that was provided.

- Be sure to have the help of a licensed mortgage professional on this. They will know more about RESPA laws and possible violations that could come in to play and help you advertise these figures correctly. This is also a great marketing opportunity for the mortgage professional. Simply state that the quotes and information are provided by: (Insert their name and contact info here.)

Going to lunch with a friend of client – Jot down some notes about lunch, where did you go, what did you eat, what did your friend or client eat? Did you enjoy it? Ask your friend or client if they enjoyed it. Can anyone guess where I am going with this? I imagine most all of you have a smart phone, right? Take a few shots of the dishes you ordered or the restaurant.

The answers to these questions are the recipe for a restaurant review. Everyone loves to go out to eat! And who knows the hot spots in town like a real estate professional? Remember the Golden Rule... Stay POSITIVE. You don't want to post a negative review on your Business page about the sushi you had for lunch. However, a good, brief review of a great place to eat can be powerful. But what does this have to do with real estate? You said that I should post content that is relevant to the housing market and posts and status updates to remind people I sell real estate. Here's what posting a brief POSITIVE restaurant review can accomplish:

- Establishes you as an expert in the local area and the neighborhood "hot spots"

- It has the potential to generate conversation and activity on your post

- It can be a segue to new opportunities to take a prospective or past client to lunch

- Help advertise local restaurants and in turn they may host your business cards on their front counter. This can be an opportunity to create another advocate for your business and someone who has a vested interest in helping you succeed!

Just recently my team posted a brief restaurant review on our Facebook Business page and it was a big success. Here's what we posted:

RESTAURANT REVIEW!!! Ted's BBQ in 5 Points!

So, the team took a field trip to Ted's BBQ today. HAD to check it out! Jincy ordered the turkey plate, Chris had smoked sausage, and Suzy had pulled pork. I was dying to try the Memphis style 'hot' tamales, so we ordered 6 and shared. Tamales were really good -- came served in the shuck. Not necessarily spicy (by my standards), but a little hot sauce fixed that. What about the rest? Chris? Jincy? Feel free to jump in here! Anybody else have an opinion on Ted's?

This review contained many great aspects of a great post. It blatantly asked for engagement, the post talked about a topic that interests almost everyone (people love BBQ) and we gave our viewers something of value: A non-biased opinion about a new restaurant in town. This post generated a lot of engaged viewers with comments about their experience and plenty of 'Likes'. What this also accomplished is association and familiarity. Chances are that every time one of our audience members drives by Ted's BBQ or sees an advertisement of some sort for Ted's, they will associate that with our Real estate team. "Oh yeah, Chris and Donna said that place was great."

Searching through the MLS – being an active real estate agent myself, I can say I do this every day. Real estate professionals have access to an abundance of information and data that is not available to the public; this is a privilege! Use this to your advantage. For example, one area of real estate that I specialize in is foreclosures and investment properties. So, I might post something like "Have you thought about investing in rental property? Believe it or not, there are some fantastic investment opportunities new on the market that you could buy for less than $500 per month! Ask me about my pick of the week! Shoot me a message with your email address and I will send a list of available investment opportunities promptly." This is a wonderful strategy for capturing the attention of eligible buyers who might not even have thought about buying a home!

Going to a closing/Closing gifts – This one is the most fun! It is easy to post positive posts, photos, and status updates right after you've gotten paid. What immediately comes to mind is to congratulate your clients, whether they are the buyer or the seller on completing the transaction. But let's take it a step further. How many of you give closing gifts to your clients? I know my team does. So here is an idea, if your clients are active Facebook users. Give them an online gift card and post it as a surprise on their Facebook page. An Amazon, Target of Walmart gift card would work great! Add a brief note with the post congratulating them on their purchase or sale. I'm not telling you to go out and spend $300 on a gift card; the amount you have budgeted is your business and in some states there is a $50 limit. But what this accomplishes is perhaps one of the most important points this book is making: REMIND PEOPLE THAT YOU ARE IN REAL ESTATE! Your clients' friends list will then see that you gave them an Amazon gift card and once they read your note, you're golden. Our goal here is trigger something in their brains. *Did my real estate professional give me a closing gift? Or,*

Wow! What a nice agent, maybe I should contact them next time we are ready to buy or sell. It is such great exposure for you and your business and creates an opportunity for referrals and meeting new clients. And it almost certainly inspires repeat business down the road from your subject clients.

Donations in lieu of closing gifts – Our town has a large number of military families, so we work with a great many Active Duty Military and Veterans. Often, we choose to make a donation in lieu of a closing gift. One of our favorite ways to say 'thank you!' to our military clients is by donating to the Wounded Warrior Project. Typically, we make a donation online through www.WoundedWarriorProject.org the day of closing. Most non-profit sites give you the option to send a snail mail notice/card to the honoree, and many now allow you to post your donation on Facebook. That unexpected acknowledgment of their service has been so well received that we have started expanding our donations to include other charities like St. Jude's Children's Hospital, the American Cancer Society and our local Humane Society.

Pay attention to what is important to your client. Are they military? Are they devoted to animal welfare? Do they have grandchildren? Has someone in their family struggled with cancer? Even if you don't have the opportunity to 'toot your own horn' by publishing your donation on Facebook, it is still a great way to show your appreciation and strengthen that important long-term relationship with your client.

People love photos! - Adding photos and videos is one of the best ways to attract your audience to visit your Business page more frequently. People love to look at pictures! That is one reason that Facebook is so popular. Social media sites have redefined the concept of a photo album. Almost everything is digital now and I doubt it will be going back to the old way.

What photos should I post? We have already discussed some ideas for the photos of your listings, homes you've sold, etc. What other photos are there? Here are some ideas for photos to post:

- Anything relevant to holidays as they happen. In the wintertime, pictures of local attractions that showcase amazing Christmas lights. On Memorial Day, share a personal story and a picture of a Veteran in your family and publicly thank them for their service and commitment. On Thanksgiving, if you support a food bank or homeless shelter, you could post photos of the facilities and ask for support from your audience. You get the point.

- Feature pictures of neighborhoods and subdivisions in areas you focus on. Something like a beautiful street that is sure to attract attention and spark interest. Don't tell your audience which neighborhood it is. Make them ask; this will spark a conversation and create engagement.

- Run a Christmas/Holiday Light Contest! Ask your Facebook friends to contribute photos of their decorations or suggest areas that are particularly festive. Award prizes – even something goofy and homemade like a tacky Christmas ornament. It's not about the prize. It's about the interaction.

Get the idea? Be creative! Keep it current and inspire interaction! Here are some other suggestions:

- Ask your Facebook friends to share photos of backyard summer fun. For instance, when I was a kid, we used to gather a collection of inflatable pools, floats, slides and hoses create our own backyard water parks.

- Ask your friends to share recipes for refreshing summer cocktails

- How about running a pumpkin carving contest the week before Halloween? Get the kids involved since people love to show off their children's efforts!

- *Borrowing listings* – (Note: *Be sure you check the real estate advertising laws in your market.*) In our market, we are allowed to borrow and advertise any listing that is held by our broker. However, we always send an email to the listing agent and ask for permission. Look through your company's inventory and find something dazzling! I call these 'bait houses' -- homes with great curb appeal at a hot (sell-able) price point. Once you receive permission, post the photo on Facebook with a short explanation. Something like, "Wouldn't you love to drive up to this gorgeous home every day? You can...Ask me how!"

Adding Videos to Facebook- Everyone is constantly telling me videos are HOT right now. I can understand where they are coming from but I do not totally agree. Good, informative, captivating, or entertaining videos are always HOT. But, just posting a new video you've created on Facebook or YouTube will not guarantee success. If you'd like to learn more about how to create good videos and use these potentially great marketing weapons correctly, I'd recommend reading **MOBILIZE YOUR CUSTOMERS** written by my co-author, John Cote. It's an Amazon.com #1 best seller and his book will provide you the information and tips to point you in the right direction. There are plenty techniques to educate you in more detail about the importance of creating videos containing high quality content. You can shoot these with your iPhone or Android phone; they have plenty of resolution and look great. Read John's book – he's brilliant!

So what kind of videos should I add to my Facebook Business page? Let's revisit what we have been discussing in this chapter. Using your daily activities to create quality content and posts. So how does this tie in with video? Well, again, what are some of the daily tasks we do as real estate practitioners? Previewing homes, putting a home on the market, going to lunch with a friend or client, searching through the MLS, or going to a closing (optimistically). Not all of these are great options for videos. I am not recommending that you tape your closings and post them online. That would probably get you sued... But closings are a great opportunity to get video testimonials from your clients! This can be as easy as taking out your smart phone and shooting a quick video of your clients praising you and your service. There is no better time since your buyer just got the keys to their new house! Your sellers may have just received a big fat check! Capture that excitement and joy and share it on video (with their permission of course.)

When putting a new home on the market, a great video option to create is a video slide show for the property. There are countless free software products that you can download from download.com or cnet.com that will allow you to create quality slide show videos. PhotoStage Slideshow Producer Professional and VideoPad Video Editor Pro are two of my favorite free options that I have used many times. Or if you currently use a virtual tour software or service, post the tour on Facebook instead.

Interview your buyers and sellers – A video interview can be such a powerful testimonial! Written testimonials can be great as well, but a video or voice recording is much more authentic. Anyone can scribble down a fake testimonial and put a fictitious name next to it online, but it's an inconvenience to try to fake a video testimonial. By the way, NEVER post a fake review. It seems obvious but it does happen. I would not take a written testimonial and create a profile to post it to either. Ask your client to do it, there are ways to get reviews posted that are ethical and will help get you more positive attention.

How about tape a short video interview with your seller(s) explaining what they love about their home. This can be a very powerful tool and this video can give your viewers a better perspective on the house than simple still photography.

Linking YouTube and Facebook accounts

Sometimes there are easier ways of doing things, and this is one of them. Some of you may already have plenty of videos on your YouTube account with great content or client testimonials. Instead of transferring and re-uploading all of these videos to Facebook, you can simply link the two accounts. Here's how:

Step 1: Log in to your Business YouTube account.

Hint: *You can log in to YouTube by going to YouTube.com or if you are already logged in to Google, using the same email address pertaining to your YouTube account, just select the YouTube option on the top menu bar. This will open a new window and you will already be logged in.*

Step 2: Look at the top of the window on the right side, you will find a small arrow pointing down directly next to the thumbnail of your profile picture. Click this arrow.

Step 3: This will expand the menu bar at the top to include a filmstrip of video categories, as well as two small columns of options on the right side. Under the YouTube Column, select YouTube settings.

Step 4: Locate the sub menu on the upper left side of the window below the YouTube logo. Select *Connected accounts*.

Step 5: Click the connect button coinciding with the first choice, Facebook.

Step 6: A pop-up window will appear a few times with YouTube asking permission to access your information, to publicly post on your behalf, and to manage your pages. Click okay, to all three.

Step 7: Now that your Facebook and YouTube accounts are connected, please notice that there are four options under *Share your public activity to connected accounts*. You have the option of sharing automatically when you upload a video, add a video to the public play list, comment on a video, or like a video.

If you select or deselect any of these buttons, click save which is located on the top right side to update your profile.

Linking Twitter and Facebook accounts. Don't do it.

Twitter can also be a powerful medium for real estate marketing. Did you know that users tweet over 400 million times per day? According to an article in The Washington Post, Twitter reported that it's now seeing over 200 million active users send 400 million tweets per day. That's a lot of status updates. So what does this have to do with Facebook? Well, the statistic you just learned is supporting evidence proving that linking your Facebook and Twitter accounts is not the best practice.

Facebook is much more personal, most people do not make it a habit of becoming friends with hundreds of people that they don't know. On Twitter, it's a whole different ball game. Twitter encourages its users to "follow" many different people, celebrities, and organizations.

Lauren Dugan, a writer for *The Unofficial Twitter Resource*, says it well, "The culture of both networks is different, so if you combine them you risk alienating your audience. By posting your tweets to your Facebook profile, you'll inundate your Facebook friends with status update after status update, taking over their newsfeed and appearing spammy." John agrees since he has tested this with his own account at www.Twitter.com/JohnCoteTV where he has over 11,000 followers as we went to print. Placing a Twitter tab into your Facebook Fan page is fine; however you don't want all of your Tweets getting posted to Facebook automatically.

Chapter 4

Customizing the tabs to showcase YOUR business. Embedding your website inside of Facebook.

What are tabs on a Facebook Business page?

One thing that is unique about Facebook Business pages compared to personal pages is the tabs feature. You may have heard these referred to as tabs or tiles but Facebook calls them tabs officially. Tabs are the small boxes that are displayed under your cover photo. By default these tabs display Photos, Map, and Likes. Sounds kind of boring, huh? Facebook offers 2 other options to add or change to if you choose: videos and notes. There is actually space for four tabs to be displayed on your page at all times even though only three are being displayed by default. Actually, until you get your first 'Like', only Photos and Map will be displayed. These tabs can be easily removed, repositioned, and organized to your liking. The tabs displayed are called your Favorites. It doesn't just stop at 4; you can actually have up to 16 tabs.

Do any of these default tabs really relate to your business? Well yes, they all *can*. The photos tab is a gateway to your Business page photo albums and the same with the videos.

Does a map showing your office and how many 'Likes' you have really represent your business? This is quite possible for some of you. Perhaps you work for a builder and you are constantly on site holding a model home open, then yes. A map of your location can be quite pertinent to *your* business. The way each agent or company does business is a little different. That is why you must customize the tabs to showcase *your* business.

'Likes' are very powerful, and displaying your number of 'Likes' can be a tremendous asset or your worst enemy. Once you get a decent number of followers on your page, boasting publicly how many 'Likes' you have can add to your credibility. 'Likes' *can* be a reflection of how many people stand behind you and your real estate business; those who appreciate your services. These people may be personal friends, acquaintances, past clients, family members, or even complete strangers that may become potential clients. From the outside looking in, each 'Like' on your page is one testimonial supporting and promoting your real estate services.

This is great and all but the number of people *Talking about this* is the true testimony. What a 'Like' accomplishes is very one-dimensional. Once a person or other Business page clicks 'Like', your Business page's posts will rarely show up on their *News Feed*. That's it! And not to mention each of them have the opportunity to hide your posts and status updates if they choose to. **Engaging** your audience is not nearly as easy, and it's exponentially more important. I will go into detail on how to accomplish the feat of engaging your audience, encouraging their participation, and producing leads later on in the book.

With all of that being said, I recommend while you are still in the early stages of building your Facebook Business page and audience to leave this tab off your top 4 which will consistently be displayed at the top of your profile page. I will not tell you to add it to the top 4 display once you hit a certain milestone in your quantity of 'Likes' because there are so many factors involved. How long has your Business page been up and running? Do you have a gigantic sphere of influence? If this is your first year in the business, chances are that your list of past clients isn't too impressive. Nor is the list of prospects in your database. But don't worry, it takes time and when you handle your database correctly, it can really pay off.

Apps on Facebook?

Did you think apps were only for smart phones and tablets? Not anymore since apps are now available on many devices, as well as social media platforms and even desktop web browsers. But for the purposes of this book, we are most interested in apps designed to be run using Facebook. The most common apps on Facebook are games. I am sure many of you remember (and still play) FarmVille. Not only was this one of the most popular game apps in Facebook history, this app became a catalyst for many developers to start creating more and more apps and games for the Facebook platform.

But what can a Facebook app do for a real estate agent or broker's Facebook Business page? Expand your content and allow your audience to learn more about you, surf your website, contact you, participate in contests, and whatever else you choose to display! On my team's Facebook Business page we display the standard photos tab, and three other custom tabs allowing users to surf different sections of our website, TourHuntsville.com without leaving Facebook. I will teach you how to do this later in this chapter.

There are many applications designed for small businesses, real estate agents, and entrepreneurs. Hundreds of companies and globally popular websites have created apps that people may use on their Facebook Business page, but many cost money and others will divert the attention of your audience away from your business and towards theirs. No wonder they are free!

Moving forward, let's focus on apps that are FREE and easy to use and customize. Most importantly apps that allow you the opportunity to showcase *your* business and capture the leads that you worked so hard to produce. To accomplish this, I mostly use an application called "iframe apps". With iframe apps, it's easy to manipulate and customize your tabs and we will go over this in more detail in the next section.

There are dozens of other apps that you can purchase for a one-time fee or a nominal monthly payment that work really well. Each has its specific purpose and if that is something you feel strongly about, we are not here to try to stop you. But the beauty of all the information, tips, and secrets we are sharing with you is that they are all 100% FREE!

iframe apps

Embedding your website inside of Facebook sounds difficult, but it's pretty straightforward. The "iframe apps" application makes it super easy to add massive amounts of content to your Facebook page. Don't worry; this is not going to get you in trouble with

Google or Bing. You are not duplicating content, and this will not negatively impact your search engine optimization. Essentially all you are doing is allowing consumers and your audience to surf through your website without leaving the comforting confines of the Facebook walls! It is a really cool concept and it works extremely well because people feel comfortable while on Facebook and you are not attempting to reroute them someplace else. Let's get started:

HINT: *Be sure that your web browser does not have a pop-up blocker activated. This will interfere with the processes to follow.*

Step 1: Be sure you are logged in to Facebook using your PERSONAL page. To load this application, it is a requirement that you do so while operating as yourself instead of your business. But don't worry; the iframes app will prompt you to choose which Business page you want to install the tab on shortly.

Step 2: Type https://www.facebook.com/iframe.apps into the space provided in your web browser. This will not log you out of your account. This is not the actual application; you've landed on iframe apps Facebook Business page.

Step 3: Click the **Go To App** button located on the right side of the screen above the four tabs displayed.

Step 4: A pop up box may appear asking for permission to access the pages you manage. Click **Ok** to proceed. A new page will appear and there will be a prompt to select a page to set up. Select your Business page. For most of you, there will be only one option to choose from. But for others that may be administrators on two or more pages, multiple options may be displayed.

Step 5: You have arrived at the SET UP MY IFRAME page. This is an opportunity to create a custom tab displaying text, images, or simply linking to your website. For this tutorial I will show you how to embed your website. This will allow your audience to browse your website without leaving Facebook.

- Fill in the *Tab name*

- Next, is *Tab image*. By default, if you do not change this image, a Welcome image will appear. Not a bad image, but definitely not custom, nor does this properly represent your website. So it is in your best interest to click **Change** and upload a custom image. HINT: *You can upload a JPG, GIF, or PNG file. The size of the image MUST be **111 x 74 pixels**.*

- Input the desired tab position. For right now, input a number between 1 and 4.

- Select the URL tab

- Type the web address (URL) for the site you would link to. In this example we are using my website, TourHuntsville.com. It is important to include the fully realized URL, starting with *http://* , which will already be displayed for your convenience.

- Do not check to keep default menu tabs. That will not be necessary for this tutorial.

- Click **SAVE**

Step 6: You will notice that nothing happened! No worries, we are not done with this screen. On the left side of the screen, locate the **Add this tab to this page** option. Click on this option.

Step 7: A pop up box will appear prompting you to choose which Facebook Page you would like to add the iframe apps custom tab to. Select the appropriate option and then click **Add Page Tab**.

Step 8: Don't be discouraged if this process doesn't turn out perfect the first time. No software is perfect, and this iframe app is no exception. If this is the case and something didn't save correctly or the picture is not displayed, then you must edit this page.

- Go to your Facebook Business page and then click on the new tab you created. This will in turn open to a new page. Your website will be displayed as well as an Admin Panel tool bar specifically for the iframe apps. HINT: *The Admin Panel will only display while you are logged in. A visitor to this page will not see the Admin Panel.*

- Click the **SET UP** icon.

- Another pop-up box will appear stating that you are using Facebook as your business page. You must *Use Facebook As* your *personal* page to proceed. Click the **Continue as (your name)** to continue.

- Now you are back at the **SET UP MY IFRAME** page. If the picture or title didn't save, redo the changes and press save.

- You may notice that everything is now in order except the Tab Name. It still displays Welcome. Quick fix: we will take care of this in this next section where we shuffle the tabs around and we will rename this new tab at that time.

Congratulations! You've created a custom tab allowing your audience to peruse your website without leaving Facebook!

Can I create more custom tabs?

You may repeat these steps to create another custom tab anytime that you would like. This particular app, iframe apps, allows you to create up to eight custom tabs. I'm sure that this should be plenty to satisfy your needs.

Now that you've created one or more custom tabs for your Facebook Business page, it is time to organize and highlight which one you wish to display as part of your top four, otherwise known as your favorites.

Step 1: Directly to the right side of the 4 tabs automatically displayed you will find a small arrow in a box that is pointing down, possibly with a number next to it. Click on this arrow.

Step 2: Move your cursor over any of the tabs displayed and a little icon of a pencil will appear. By clicking this icon, you will be able to swap tab positions, change or remove the tabs, remove from favorites, edit the tab's name or picture, and even create a custom URL for that tab.

Rearranging the tabs on your Facebook Business page is a great way to keep your page fresh. This will possibly attract the attention of your audience more often because they will notice something is different. Change the order of your tabs regularly and also you may want to add new tabs periodically.

Are there other apps available to create custom tabs?

There are actually dozens of apps to choose from to create custom tabs where you can run promotions and contests on your Facebook Business page. They can also be used to embed your YouTube channel, Twitter feed, Pinterest or Instagram accounts, reviews, rewards, contests, surveys, fan gates and more. Not all of the options out there are free, but here are a couple more that work very well and are either free or very inexpensive. You can always search Google for more options.

Woobox- This app company has a great interface that is very popular and easy to use. It will handle all of the tabs I mentioned previously and it also does many similar things to iframe apps. The biggest difference with Woobox is that you can create a custom tab that links to your website outside of Facebook. With iframes, you are actually embedding your site to allow visitors to surf without leaving Facebook. Woobox does that as well, but gives you both options to choose from. To learn more about this app visit their website at Woobox.com.

Tabfoundry- This is another option for you to choose from when making custom tabs for your Facebook Business page. They do have a free version but it is very limited. This app offers three packages including tech support and unlimited custom tabs for unlimited Facebook pages. That service is not for everyone, but I wanted to let you know it's out there for a minimal monthly fee. To find out more about Tabfoundry, visit TabFoundry.com or simply search the term Tabfoundry in your Facebook search bar.

Heyo- Heyo.com (formerly Lujure.com) offers a wide variety of choices as well although all of them are paid. They do offer a free trial.

What is a Fan gate?

Some experts believed at one point in time that Fan gates were the most effective way to get someone to 'Like' your Fan page once they visit it. Okay, so what is it? The Social Media Examiner defines Facebook Fan-gating as the process of "creating two versions of a tab on a page, one that's shown to users who already Like your page and one to those who have not Liked the page." You may have heard of the term "like-gating", which is referring to the same thing. Tens of thousands of Business and Fan pages have been and still are using this method because it works! Creating a custom Fan gate can be accomplished by using any of the websites we mentioned to create one. We recommend testing it with and without to see how it affects your click through rate (CTR) and decide whether or not you need one.

Chapter 5

Build your audience.

What good is a performance without an audience? It's not. There are many definitions for the word audience, and they all practically say the same thing. Dictionary.com hosts my favorite version: *a regular public that manifests interest, support, enthusiasm, or the like; a following*. Your audience on Facebook is exactly that. Referencing what I have mentioned earlier in this book, *each 'Like' on your page is one testimonial supporting and promoting your real estate services*. That's wonderful. So how do I get more 'Likes'?

I've used the term *audience* several times in this book and it refers to the people who 'Like' your Facebook Business page. Let's clarify a few things. Your page may have 1000 'Likes' but that doesn't matter. This is an outlandish statement isn't it? Am I confusing you yet? I am about to encourage you to get more likes and even show you how, step by step. But I am telling you that it doesn't matter? That is correct.

Having a million 'Likes' would be lovely, but the real number that matters is the one that comes after the 'Likes'. "*89 Talking about this*" is what is most important. But you have to crawl before you can walk; in context, first build your audience of 'Likes' then work on getting them to talk about you.

Who not to invite – Your competitors

Imagine one of your competitors introduced a new way to do business and they are experiencing great success! Would they just hand over the secret recipe? NO! Why would you? Inviting and allowing your competitors to be a part of your audience is exactly that. By reading this book, you are learning innovative, creative techniques and approaches to increasing your sales and revenue using Facebook. So why would you openly invite your competitors to come check out what you are doing? It is a good point to make that if someone wants to snoop and discover how you are marketing your Business of Facebook, they can. But, don't make it too easy.

There can be the argument that it is beneficial to have other real estate professionals in your audience to give your listings more exposure. This is true, but the benefits of not including your competitors outweigh this exponentially.

Two childhood games come to mind when I think about success: Copy Cat and Follow the Leader. Most people want to be successful, but when new technologies arise few will know how to do so on their own. The point I am trying to make is that people model themselves after successful people. It can be considered an honor or even flattering when people emulate you and your actions, but don't hand your competitors an invitation to do so.

John wanted to offer another side to this discussion; adopt an abundance mindset. By purchasing this book and implementing the strategies learned you have created a marketing advantage over most other real estate agents in your area. If you freely share this information and help other agents, some of them will return the favor by bringing you referrals and business. They will know what your target market is and that may not be their specialty among many other reasons. Peter Diamandis wrote a great book called *ABUNDANCE* that we suggest you read which covers that mindset in detail.

Invite friends from your personal page

Not to harp upon the importance of linking your personal and Business pages together yet again, but it is that important. Facebook makes it very easy to invite your friends from your personal page to 'Like' your Business page. Here's how:

Step 1: Ensure you are logged in to Facebook and then click to use Facebook as your Business page.

Step 2: Locate the section titled Invite Friends in the Admin Panel above your cover photo.

HINT: *If you find yourself searching for the Admin Panel, it is always located above your cover photo. If it is not displaying, don't worry. There is a small button on the top right corner of your Business profile page that either says Hide or Show. If the button displays Show, then click it and your Admin Panel should reappear. Of course this is not true while you are logged in.*

Step 3: Facebook will import your friends list for you and display a thumbnail of his/her profile pictures and his/her name with an option to Invite or X (Remove). If you choose to invite them, simply click Invite and an invitation for them to 'Like' your page will appear in their notification center.

HINT: *Be sure that your Business page's profile picture and name allows your potential audience to know it's your business and not something spammy.*

Invite friends from the personal page of each admin of your Business page

Each administrator of your Business page will also be given the opportunity to invite his/her personal friends list as well. So be sure to encourage them to do so. His/her contact list will import automatically as well while they are logged in and using Facebook as your Business page. Have them follow the instructions above from the section **Invite friends from your personal page**.

Import email contacts from each of your email addresses and your administrator's email addresses

Chances are, as a real estate professional, you have emailed back and forth with hundreds if not thousands of people. The wonderful thing is that your email provider, whom ever you use, saves all of these contacts for you, or at least their email addresses. This list of email addresses is an amazing opportunity to invite large quantities of people to 'Like' your page. Here's how to do it:

Step 1: At the very top of the Admin Panel, on the right end you will see a drop down icon called *Build Audience*. Click on it. Then select *Invite Email Contacts*.

Step 2: A list of commonly used email providers will be displayed in a new pop up window. To the right of each option will be an opportunity to click Invite Contacts. Click this button corresponding with the appropriate email provider.

HINT: *If your email provider is not listed, click Other Email Service and then type in your email address and password. If you use Microsoft Outlook, Thunderbird, or some other similar product click the Other Tools option.*

Step 3: After authenticating your log in information, you will next see a list of all of your email contacts. There is an option to select/deselect all at the top, but I do not recommend you invite everyone. Remember, inviting your competitors is of no value to you. Be sure to go through each and every contact meticulously and make sure you weed out the competition before pressing *Preview Invitation* at the bottom right corner of the window.

Step 4: Review the invitation to ensure that everything is correct. Before clicking *Send* at the bottom, be sure to check the box to the left agreeing to: *I am authorized to send invitations to the email addresses I've imported.*

Advertise your Facebook URL on all of your materials

What other advertising methods do you use? Hopefully a wide variety! I am referring to everything you put your name on. Business cards, emails, property fliers, your website and direct mail campaigns to name a few. Advertise your Facebook Business page on all of these! Referencing Chapter 2, you learned that each Facebook Business page has its own unique URL or web address. Most likely something similar to http://facebook.com/MaryJamesSellsHomes. Include your Facebook Business page's specific web address on all of your ads.

Is this going to increase your Business page's audience? Probably not significantly at first, it's not that easy. Increasing your audience is not a magic trick. It takes a little effort and some incentive to encourage prospects to 'Like' your page.

Incentivize people to "like" your page

Giving something away doesn't always mean you must spend money. It is, however nearly a necessity to give some sort of an incentive for people to take action. Here is what I suggest. Don't print or type just your unique Facebook URL on all of your advertisements and handouts. Also include an incentive, something that will spring the reader into action! Easier said than done, right? The thought of what to give away can be over-whelming. You may be saying to yourself, "What do I have containing value to give away that people will want?"

Having a real estate license is truly a privilege. You are entrusted with information that is not readily available to the public. You can use it to create free reports for target neighborhoods. I am not in any way saying to start distributing sold and proprietary information to anyone who will take it. But offer a free report individualized to the reader. Don't get me wrong; giving away something much bigger that does have monetary value is also a great way to entice future prospects to 'Like' your page. A higher value incentive typically leads to more likes.

For example your advertisement could say:

'Like' us on Facebook and you will receive a free custom Market Analysis to show you your home's value! Facebook.com/MaryJamesSellsHomes. Or;

'Like' us on Facebook and you will be entered to win a Free iPod Touch! Mary James, REALTOR® Facebook Business Page (URL linked)

HINT: *It is important to note that this method is fantastic for getting lots of 'Likes', but not necessarily the best approach for targeting a specific demographic or people who are actually interested in buying or selling a house.*

Chapter 6

Assigning admins and advocates for my business and my success. Importance of asking for help from people who want to see you succeed.

Facebook can be one of the greatest tools available for a real estate professional to ask for referrals. Many people in your sphere of influence are most likely already on Facebook; why not use it to your advantage? The key is learning how to engage these people and transform them into advocates for your business! Teach them the concept of edification and ask for their help and support.

Advocates and Edification

Let's define a few terms: To *edify* is to instruct or improve a person morally or intellectually. For instance, if someone is edifying you, they are praising you to someone else. Perhaps by informing them of your successes or how wonderful of a parent you are. The Merriam-Webster Dictionary defines *advocate* as a person who publicly supports or recommends a particular cause or policy.

Edification

Edification is a very powerful concept. If I told you that I was fantastic parent, would you believe me? Probably not, because it simply appears that I am being boastful. But if someone else you know and trust tells you that I am a fantastic parent, you are more apt to believe that it's true. Can you see how the process of edification can be so powerful?

When I was a younger man, my step-dad, Rob enlightened me on the concept of edification. He did this to try to snap me out of a phase I was going through – basically, I was a pretty cocky 15 year old. Of course I didn't see it, but evidently others were aware. Rob taught me that I should stop focusing on how cool I am or my athleticism, and focus on telling others wonderful things about other people. So that is exactly what I did. My new mission in life was to share sincerely positive things about others daily to everyone. Wow! It was amazing how much happier I was and how popular I became. I took the focus off of me and instead focused on building up others. Hold on with me, we will get to how this relates soon

Advocates for my business

I'll take two please! Just kidding, I actually am extremely blessed to have many advocates in my life. These people support me in my business and my life, which helps me succeed every day. Let's face it; in the real estate business it can be feast or famine, and sometimes one more than the other. This profession is a roller coaster ride with a plethora of credit card debt at times and then within 30 days you could be swimming in dough. Have you ever thought about how much advocates for your business can help you balance your productivity and income? One way to think about these advocates for your business are those who send you referrals.

In a perfect world, your business would be completely referral based. But most of us aren't there yet. Many of you probably have to rely on new leads from the Internet, advertisements, or sitting open houses. There is nothing wrong with these methods of getting new business, but there are other ways to get business and from my experience, receiving referrals is among the easiest. If you are a newer agent or someone just getting back in the game, referrals are probably not a large portion of your lead generation. With that being said, you are not necessarily doing anything wrong, but what would make people want to refer you business automatically? This is why you need to ASK for referrals! Engage the people within your sphere of influence thus creating advocates for your business.

I can remember a few instances when I was struggling financially and a few referrals from my friends and past clients bailed me out. This past January, my team was having a rough month. One by one, we had three deals fall through. Two were due to financing and one because the buyer changed his mind after the election and decided

54

not to buy. Like most of you, we have overhead. We have to pay our assistant, office dues, and many other miscellaneous expenses. Losing those three contracts REALLY hurt. It was definitely not the way we wanted to start out the New Year. I had $85 in my checking account and the bills kept coming in. And people think that all real estate agents and brokers live a glamorous lifestyle. Does this sound like you sometimes?

Let's get back to the story. My funnel was draining and I barely had any deals inside. It seemed like the end was near. Then something amazing happened! One message on Facebook turned everything around. All it took to pull us out of the quicksand was one referral from a very appreciated advocate. "Hey Chris, I have a friend moving into town from Charlotte and he's in a hurry to buy and get moved. Do you think that you could help him?" You can use your imagination to guess what my answer was. This past client of mine was truly an advocate for my business, simply because we had helped him purchase his first home a few months back. After closing I mentioned to him to *please* keep my team in mind if he came across anyone looking to buy or sell a home. Not only did he send us a referral, he also left us a wonderful testimonial on our Trulia profile and our Facebook Business page!

Do you see the importance of having advocates in your life that edify you and your real estate services on a daily basis? But, where do you find advocates? Often they are right in front of you; perhaps you haven't engaged them in the action of edifying you to others. I'm sure that many of you have lots of past clients that you haven't stayed in touch with. Following up isn't always a real estate agent's strong point, I know. It can be quite difficult sometimes, and we all try to have systems in place (CRM) to keep track of everything. No licensee is perfect, but you could be losing potential advocates every time you lose touch with one of your past clients or friends. Facebook is arguably *the* best way to keep these people engaged in your life and keep you in their mind.

You might be thinking, "Where do I start engaging the advocates in my life? Where do I find such people? And how do I use Facebook to ask for and receive referrals?" Start by asking yourself a few other questions:

- Who do I know that *really* wants to see me succeed?

- Which of my past and current clients could I ask for referrals?

- Which people in my life are already advocates for my business?

- Are these people on my friends list on Facebook? Are they fans of my Facebook Business page?

Make a list of people for each question. This is your starting point. How many of these people, whether it is your friend, your mom or past clients that you sold a house to 9 months ago, have you asked to refer you business? How many of them have you asked to simply remember you if they hear of someone who is in the market to buy or sell? This isn't a hard concept, but unfortunately that is not how we are wired.

Growing up, I am sure that many of you were taught to be independent. "Don't ask for help, you can do it yourself!" Sometimes it's almost as if it is impolite to ask for help or for a recommendation. I am here to tell you to step away from those teachings and set your pride aside. Selling real estate is no place for such thinking.

'I can do it on my own" doesn't always work well in this business, and that thought process can get lonely and exhausting. Sure, you *could* run your entire business by generating Internet leads, but what happens when the leads run out? So do your closings and commission checks. Ask for help!

Identify your advocates and engage them!

Now it's time to implement what you've just learned about *advocates* and *edification*.

Step 1: Examine your sphere of influence and audience and pick out your current advocates.

Let's take a look at your friends list on your personal page as well as your congregation of 'Likes' on your Facebook Business page. Start by picking out at least 5 people from these lists that certainly are advocates for your business. Thank them immediately. Log on to your Facebook Business page right now and send each one of them a private message. Something like this will work:

"Hi _____, I hope you are doing well! I was just thinking about you and how much I appreciate your support and friendship. Thank you for believing in me and supporting me in my career. I appreciate that you keep me in mind when you hear of someone in the market to buy or sell property. Look forward to seeing you soon! Thanks, (your name)."

Feel free to use the above example verbatim. Sending this message accomplishes quite a few things. Most importantly, you are able to sincerely portray your appreciation and gratitude to those who already support you and actively edify you and your services on a regular basis. Also, this reinforces and reengages your advocates and reminds them to continue to support you. Studies have shown that when people feel appreciated, they are much more apt to continue performing acts of kindness.

Step 2: Compile a list of people that you have not yet engaged

Next, go back to your friends list and 'Likes' on your Facebook Business page and pick out 10 people that you have never asked for a referral. If you cannot find 10, either you are really good about asking for referral business with everyone you know or you don't have many people on your friends list. Either way, jot down as many as you can find.

Again, stop what you are doing right now and send each one of them a private Facebook message. Below I will provide another example, which you are free to use and plug in the appropriate details.

"Hi _____, I hope you are doing well! I was just thinking about you and how much I appreciate your support and friendship. Thank you for believing in me and supporting me in my career. Will you please keep me in mind when you hear of someone in the market to buy or sell property? I'd be

honored to assist them with their real estate needs. I truly appreciate you! We should get together soon. Thanks, (your name)."

As you have probably already noticed, this script is very similar to the first one. Instead of thanking them for referring your business, now you are asking them to refer business to you. Once again, this is engaging them. Using words like please and appreciate make people feel good; it's nourishment for the soul. ALWAYS insert these powerful words in every message and conversation you have with your advocates or potential advocates.

Step 3: Assigning administrators for your Facebook Business page

There is a big difference between engaging past clients, friends, and acquaintances to refer your business, and entrusting them to help you manage your Facebook Business page. People with the ability to manipulate, add to, or change your page should be hand-picked and chosen wisely. So who is a good candidate for this position?

- Your spouse or significant other

- Your teenage children who have a firm grasp of Facebook

- Your assistant if you have one, or if you operate within a team or group, one of the other members

- A close friend who you know you can trust

Now that you have your administrators picked out, the next step is to make it official.

Step A: Make sure you are logged in and you have selected to *Use Facebook As* your Business page.

Step B: Once you are on your Business profile page, locate the *Get More Likes* section. This is located above your cover photo in the *Admin Panel*.

Step C: To the right of the *Get More Likes* title, click on See Likes. This will pop up a new window.

Step D: The new window will display a list of all of the people who 'Like' your Facebook Business page, to the right of each person's name and picture is the button named *Make Admin*.

Step E: Press *Make Admin* for the list of people you have picked out.

Step F: You will now find yourself on the administrator page. This page will show all the admins for your site. Directly below the name of each administrator, you will see the *role* that has been assigned.

By default whomever you just appointed as an admin will show up as a *Manager*. Click on the word *Manager* and a drop down list will appear allowing you to assign different *roles* for your administrators. Choose the appropriate role that corresponds with what you would like them to have access to and what duties they will be performing.

This should do the trick. There are other ways to assign one or multiple audience members as administrators on your page by going through the **Edit Page** drop down menu located at the top of the Admin Panel. Simply click on Manage Admin Roles.

HINT: *Just a reminder, you can always check and see which account you are using by looking up in the upper right corner of the screen. Here you will find a small thumbnail picture and the name of the profile.*

HINT: *Make sure you discuss this with whom you pick and ask them for their assistance.*

Step 4: Delegating posting tasks and working together to accomplish great results.

Assigning administrators for your account doesn't do any good unless your newly appointed advocate administrators participate! Delegating is an essential task for anyone in a management role and that is exactly what you are. Your business is the face of the Business page, and you should maintain control of what is posted. To many of you, the logical solution would be to just get it done yourself. If you want something done right, you have to do it yourself, right? As you probably know, that is not always the answer. Individuals can accomplish great things, but teams can typically accomplish much more.

Hats that a page admin can wear

Each page administrator can have a different role assigned to them: Manager, Content Creator, Moderator, Advertiser, and Insights Analyst. You can choose which role to assign depending on what they need to work on or have access to. Visit https://www.facebook.com/help/323502271070625/ for more information.

HINT: *Remember, at any point you can click on Manage Admin Roles under the Edit Page drop down list at the top of the Admin Panel. This will allow you to change the assigned roles of your admins as well as add or delete administrators as you see fit.*

Start by analyzing your appointed administrators. One person may be really interested in live music or local events and attractions. Use their passions and interests to strengthen your page. Consult with this person and assign them the task of posting 3 times per week about upcoming events, concerts, and shows. Incidentally, you can hire a company to do your posting for you, however they will not have as good a handle on your brand DNA or personality as you will. My assistant and I do all of my posting and we have had great success in just a few minutes a day.

We don't recommend you use your kids to do your posts for you, no matter how much time they spend on Facebook. Although they may be experts at using Facebook for personal use, it's completely different for business use. There will be exceptions of course, but in general it's not worth the risk of a teen posting something that they think is funny which adults do not find interesting or amusing. As a social media expert and marketing consultant, John has seen many examples of poorly run Facebook campaigns where the business owner did not understand how to use it and they let their kids run it for them. More often than not the results were not good.

Posting on your Facebook Business page must become habitual to consistently achieve great results. I can't begin to tell you how many times I have been told, "Marketing on Facebook doesn't work, I tried it." Well, how long did you keep it up? What were you posting? Did you actively engage your audience and offer incentives rewarding participation? Most likely you didn't. Repetition is key and you need to instill this thought process with your administrators. There are plenty of REALTORS® just like me who are closing deals using Facebook and you can too.

Chapter 7

What should I post?
Promoted Posts and Facebook Ads.

What is a post?

This blog post at http://blog.scripted.com/writers/what-is-a-facebook-post/ says it best: "A Facebook post or 'status update' is a message in a special delivery cyber-bottle. It's a comment, picture or other media that is posted on the user's Facebook page or wall." That pretty much sums it up. Think of it this way, a post or status update is a chance to share something specific with your audience or group of friends at any given time.

A little deeper into this article, the author shared a list of "7 qualities of a Bangin' Facebook post!" I have similar thoughts with a few differences so here's the 5 "Must Haves" in a Facebook post that I live by:

1. Headlines that not only attract attention, but capture and inform

2. Ask a question that makes your audience stop and think then reply

3. Keep it clear, concise and appropriate for your target audience

4. Give away something of value

5. A Call to Action; encourage them to take the next step

Headlines that not only attract attention but that capture and inform. What does this mean? Think of a headline as the *title* of your post or status update. Draw the reader into the post; entice them to read it all. Most people skim while reading, so your headline has only an instant to capture your reader's attention. Remember, great headlines attract attention, select an audience, and deliver a complete message.

Ask a question that makes your audience stop and think, then reply. Asking questions is an extremely effective way to engage members of your audience. People love to be asked questions because subconsciously this makes them feel like their opinions are valued and important. Make sure the questions you ask are answerable rather than rhetorical. *"What is the meaning of life?"* is too esoteric (*it's 42 btw.*) Answers to your posted questions are engagement and this is what we are trying to accomplish with any post. Leads on Facebook come from an engaged audience.

Keep it clear, concise and appropriate for your target audience. When writing a post or status update think about *whom* you are writing to. Who is your specific audience? Some posts may not apply to your entire collection of 'Likes' and others might. Be sure to keep this in mind. A good post or status update should never feel like a novel! Short, concise, yet complete posts are what you should strive for. I have read that posts should not exceed 200 words, and somewhere else I heard that up to 300 is okay. My model does not have a specific rule to follow regarding word count, simply keep in mind that if your post is too long for you to read, it's most likely going to be a hassle for your audience as well.

Give away something of value. Often people mistake the phrase, "something of value," with a dollar amount. Not necessarily. Rarely does this have anything to do with you spending money. Remember when I talked about using the perks of holding a privileged real estate license to your advantage? As a real estate pro, you are entrusted with so much information and some of you may have access to sold data or special training that you can share. Use this to your advantage! We like to say that this is an opportunity to show off your "mad real estate skills." Offer a free market analysis in your posts. Create a blog or article talking about the *TOP 3 qualities in a house that buyers are looking for.* Explain technical and industry exclusive terminology to educate your audience. Sometimes people see acronyms like PPSQFT, CMA, SS, etc. and aren't quite sure what they mean. Be the source!

Call to action; encourage them to take the next step. In general, humans don't take the leap or the next step on their own. You have to encourage them; give them a push if you will. Calls to action are quite possibly the most important aspect of sales, whether you are selling homes or pizzas. A call to action challenges the reader to take the next step and what the next step is, is up to you. If a call to action is constructed correctly, you, the writer, are in control. You control the outcome of the reader's actions; here are a few actions you may want your readers to take.

- Click on a link that takes them to *your* website to search for homes for sale.

- Contact you via email, telephone, or text.

- Download a free report

- Comment on a post answering a question or sharing a story

- Watch a video that will inform and intrigue them to learn more

Post Types

There are seven types of posts that you can create on your Facebook Fan or Business page. Facebook allows you to choose from the first six in the new post area on your page. *Status, Photo/Video*, and *Offer, Event* + will appear at the top of the posting area. To choose *Milestone* or *Question* you must click the *Offer, Event* + tab to see these options. I will go over each one in detail below.

HINT: *These six post types are available and displayed on the desktop version of Facebook. Currently this feature is not available from a mobile device. Facebook's mobile app only allows you to "Write Post" or "Share Photo." While accessing FB through a mobile web browser you may see "Update Status" as an option instead of "Write Post." Keep in mind that you can add links in your posts along with photos or videos as well. You can even add photos into your comments on status updates now.*

Status- Facebook auto-populates the status update area posting the question: *What have you been up to?* That doesn't mean that you must use this section as you traditionally would on a personal account. That is merely Facebook's suggestion of what you should write. For your Business or Fan page, this is a blank slate. Be sure to read Chapter 10 where you will receive 101 great posts and status updates to drive engagement.

Photos/Videos- By clicking on the *Photos/Videos* tab you will have two options: Upload Photos/Video or Create Photo Album. If you would like to share multiple photos at one time in a post you must create a photo album. Be sure to label the album appropriately as well as fill in the pertinent information about what the album is representing or displaying. To share the photo album in a post once it has been created, click on photos, then albums and select the album you wish to share. Just like a post or photo, under the body of the post find the share button. This will then allow you to share the album on your page.

Offer- This post type is not necessarily something that you will need to use as a Real Estate Professional. *Offer* allows your Business or Fan page to highlight a product or products that you sell. *In Store Only, In Store & Online*, and *Online Only* are the three options you can choose from. I will go over this type of post in more detail during our weekly video training series at **SocialMarketingTV.com** to show you how you can use *Offer* to attract new business and educate consumers.

Event- Holding an open house this weekend? Is your company hosting a charity event? Use the *Event* post type to display to your audience. Simply click *Event* and fill out the appropriate information. You will be able to input: Name, Details, Where, Tickets, and When. *Events* will show up on your timeline and it is in your best interest to *Share* this event a few times leading up to the date and time to remind your audience it is coming up.

Milestone- This is another one that is not on the top of my list of posts to do. A milestone by definition is *an action or event marking a significant change or stage in development*. By posting a *Milestone* on your FB Business page, you are highlighting this event or occurrence for everyone to see. Examples of a *Milestone* post could be getting your real estate license, selling your first home, getting your broker's license, opening your own company, winning awards, etc. These will stay on your *timeline* permanently unless you remove them. Using *Milestones* can highlight how long you have been in business and can add to your credibility.

Question- This is an opportunity to poll your audience. When using the *Question* post type, you will be prompted to ask something. Then below you will find a button labeled *add poll options*. This is where you list the array of answers to the question you are asking. For example, let's pretend the question posted is "What is your favorite style of home?" Under poll options you would add a few or several different construction types: Craftsman, Traditional, Bungalow, Mid-Century Post Modern, Brick Rancher, etc. The post will show the question and below the answers you have added. Your audience will be allowed to choose one answer and Facebook will keep track of the tally for each answer. This is a great way to get feedback from your audience and followers and to make them feel involved and that you value their opinions.

Share- You can share just about anything on your page. If you find a really cool article online and the author or website has provided you with a *Share on Facebook* button, click the button and you will then have the option to share the article on your page. Another case could be while you are browsing another Fan page or personal page and you would like to share someone's status update, picture or video they have posted on *your* Business page. Below the post, directly to the right of the *Comment* button, click *Share*. A pop up window will appear. If you are *Using Facebook As* your Business page, then the post will, by default, be posted on the timeline of your business profile page. If you are *Using Facebook As* your personal page, you can choose to share the photo *On your own timeline, On a friend's timeline, In a group, On a page you manage, or In a private message.*

Who sees my posts?

Posts are only seen by 10% of your audience on average and not all of them will notice it. This is due to EdgeRank; the algorithm that

Facebook uses to determine what appears in their users' news feeds. EdgeRank not only determines which of your connections (interactions with your friends and fans) is the most important to you, but also which kinds of content (posts) should appear ranked higher than others.

There are many factors that affect the EdgeRank of each post or status update you create. Posts with more interactions with multiple users and engagement hold a higher weight and are more apt to show up on more of your audience member's *News Feeds*. The ultimate goal is to get your posts and status updates to show up higher and more often. Strive to create posts that stimulate interaction and engage as many of your audience members as possible. Be sure to read and feel free to use any of the *101 great posts and status updates to drive engagement* that you will find in Chapter 10.

Promoted Posts

EdgeRank determines how many people will see your post...unless you pay to promote it. Facebook describes promoted posts as *an easy way to get more people to see your posts. Promoted posts appear higher in News Feed, so there's a better chance your audience will see them.* This is a different type of ad unit and it basically means you're getting your posts promoted to a far larger audience (all of your friends or fans and most of their friends) as opposed to less than 10% when you typically make a post. You can track these numbers in detail from inside your Facebook Ad account. When you click on the "Promote this post" link, it will show you about how many people will "see" the post. Not everyone will notice it of course, that is just the number of people who have the post show up on their timeline.

When you click on "Boost this Post" you can geo-target specific demographics (for example by selecting these attributes: business owner, lives within 20 miles of 90210, entrepreneur, etc) who are not connected to you currently which can create a highly targeted ad. You can literally target a single individual by name or an entire business if, for example, they were relocating all of their employees to your area.

So how much does it cost? Good question. Facebook goes on to explain *that the cost to promote a post depends on several factors; including your geographic location and how many people you're reaching. Click Promote to see how much your post will cost to promote.* Every post can be different and this is a time to reflect on what I have already told you about Facebook. Facebook is constantly changing and they have teams in place whose sole purpose is to constantly improve their systems and the user experience.

The cost to promote a post and how the price is calculated has already changed a few times since the spring of 2012 when "Promoting" was introduced. With that being said, the pricing scheme will likely change again and again as time goes on. The important question here is this: **Does promoting a post work?** The short answer is, yes it does, when implemented properly. The cool part is that it's very cheap to test it out; you can get started for only $5.

There are so many variables at play and each of you runs your business differently. Each post or status update you create may have different goals and calls to action in mind. Promoting a post with a survey about a new interior-decorating project your seller is working on would be a great post to pay for promoting. Many people are interested in decorating and this gives your audience an opportunity to share their opinions. But, promoting a post such as, "We wish you all a Happy Monday!" will not get you the return on investment you are looking for.

The premise of this book relies on marketing your business for FREE on Facebook. Promoted posts are not free, and I am in no way telling you that you must use this method to succeed. I will tell you however, that it works. The main objective of promoting a post is to increase its reach and to get on more people's News Feeds; that is exactly what it does. If you are going to promote posts, be sure to do so selectively.

My experience with promoting posts has been up and down. Just like anything else in life and in marketing, trial and error enhances the learning curve. My team has used Facebook's "Promote Your Post" a few times and we have experienced much higher reach with each post we promoted. The ROI (return on investment) was not stellar on every post, but for the most part we feel our selection of which post to promote set the stage for the outcome.

When I first heard about promoting posts I decided to give it a try. I used my post, "Congratulations to Jim and Barbara on their new home! We are very happy for you and glad that we were able to serve you and your real estate needs! Welcome home." I added a snapshot of their new home then promoted the post for $10. I was pleased to see that it reached over one thousand viewers and received a few shares. But, after reflecting on what I had accomplished, as you can guess, the reality set in. What good did that really do? I did not get any leads from posting this and was paying to promote it. Was it a complete failure or waste of money? Maybe, but I accomplished something HUGE! I was able to remind one thousand people that I was selling real estate. As I tried this method a few more times, I found myself using promoted posts more effectively.

Facebook Ads

I don't utilize Facebook Ads in my advertising beyond small tests, but this can be a powerful way to promote your business. Facebook ads are very similar to Google ads, which you see every time you do a Google search. They appear on the top and right side of every Google search page. Bing.com and other search websites have the same set up to create ad revenue. Facebook ads that appear on the right side have an extremely low click through rate, even when compared to Google ads.

We use Facebook ads several times a year for small campaigns and testing. It does take time to test and track the campaign, change the images and headlines, track again and so on. Facebook ads do work, but as I mentioned, we have had better results with free status updates. As with promoted posts, we have received mixed results. The targeting capabilities of the ads are very impressive and they are inexpensive to try out, however the click-through-rate (CTR) is very low. There are plenty of courses and tutorials online that teach how to use and optimize Facebook ads.

Until July of 2013, Facebook had the "20% rule" which stated in their terms of service that your images needed to be less than 20% text. This was to prevent an ad that basically had only text in the image to supplement the text that was allowed next to the image. Although they have lifted that restriction, we recommend you try to stay close to those numbers when you place your image in the ad. The ad will have a higher CTR if is has a compelling image. The actual ad text is limited to 25 characters for the headline then 90 characters for content. The also get a line for your domain name link. We understand the desire to add more text in the image, but it lowers CTR's almost every time.

A relatively new alternative ad is called retargeting. This service is now available for Facebook ads; they have been popular for a few years on Google Adwords. What retargeting does is follow a visitor to your site and serve them your ads on other websites that participate. For example, if a person goes to your website at YourRealtySite.com, then visits ESPN.com, they will see an ad for your company. If they then go to USATODAY.com they would see the same ad (or another one of your ads) there as well. Now you can pay to have people who visit then leave your website see your ads on Facebook. We have not tested retargeting on Facebook yet but it works really well with Google Adwords when you have a well-optimized campaign with a good call to action. As we continue to implement, test and track online ads you can stay up to date on our Fan page at Facebook.com/RealEstateMarketingBook.

#Hashtags on Facebook

As we were getting ready to publish this book, Facebook announced the implementation of hashtags into their user interface. For those of you using Twitter, Google+, Tumblr and Instagram, this is a common part of the experience and many feel it's actually quite overdue for Facebook. For those of you who are unfamiliar with the use of hashtags, we'll explain it briefly. The "pound" sign (#) is known as the "hashtag" in social media circles. Chris Messina, an open source software advocate, has been credited with introducing the hashtag to Twitter according to Wikipedia. Many of the major social media sites have adopted the hashtag as a method to search for posts referring to similar information or events.

By placing the hashtag symbol in front of the word or phrase, users who are searching for a particular topic or category can find it much more easily. This action creates a clickable link that will take you to the most recent posts in the site (Facebook in this case) that are using that hashtag. You cannot use spaces when creating a hashtag so all of the words must be together. Using upper or lower case does not matter for creating the link however many people capitalize each word to make it easier to read. We prefer to capitalize the first letter of each word but either method works fine. Hashtags created on other social media sites like Twitter and Instagram that are shared on Facebook will have their links clickable and searchable when posted or shared.

Hashtags allow the user to find posts that have topics of interest to them. Think of it as a search engine for a keyword or phrase. Some national examples include topics like #NBAFinals, #Superbowl, #AmericanIdol, #MadMen, #BostonStrong, #Election, #NSA or #Petraeus. By the way, abbreviations in hashtags are very common. You can do things like #LARealEstate or #SDrealestate instead of spelling out the entire city name. Anyone can create a hashtag for any topic and post with it. This allows your post to reach a far wider audience than just your friends or fans and their friends. Anyone who searches for that hashtag can find your post. For some, that is a terrifying prospect. As a marketer (and you are a marketer) this is exactly what you want.

During the "Arab Spring" of 2011, Twitter became one of the leading conduits of up to the second information regarding the political and social upheaval that was occurring in multiple Middle Eastern countries. Citizen journalists in these countries were posting updates with #ArabSpring to keep the world informed and it eventually led to several authoritarian governments being overthrown. Regardless of your political or religious beliefs, it was a powerful demonstration of the value and reach of social media.

As an example for someone marketing in real estate, you could post on Facebook about an open house in a particular area or neighborhood then add a hashtag of the location. This will help

72

people looking for open houses that weekend to find your post whether or not they are friends or fans. It would look like this: #CoralGablesOpenHouse. You could also do it separately as #CoralGables #OpenHouse. Alternatively, something with a wider appeal like the name of your city with "real estate" at the end, would look like this: #MiamiRealEstate. This allows you send your message out to as broad or highly targeted a group as you wish.

Go ahead and search for some of these hashtags on Facebook (just type it into the search bar on the top of the page) and include searches for your city to see some examples of how real estate professionals are using this locally and nationally. Don't limit your searches to real estate, look for #refinance, #roofing, #plumbing, #landscaping or anything connected to real estate to see how they are integrating hashtags. When you find some that are getting shares and comments, deconstruct why it's working and copy them!

Be creative and test out a variety of them to see which ones get the best response. Every post you make should end with at least one hashtag to help get it found and shared more frequently. You can post as many hashtags as you want so feel free to add several or more which are relevant to your post. Since you are not limited in Facebook to a small number of characters, this is your chance to test a wide variety of hashtags. When talking about anything other than real estate, like events or topics, post them with hashtags as well to help broaden your reach. Try posting a hashtag with only your city name and see what the traffic looks like to your post. You can be advertising an open house, a new listing, or just talking about current events.

Do some research and find out what other real estate professionals are using in your area. This won't take much time to get popular everywhere; it's already catching on in larger cities. If you jump right on it and start posting a lot of relevant material with hashtags, you have the first mover advantage. You may find your posts are the only ones using that hashtag which is great if Facebook users are searching for it. Eventually your competition will catch on but now is a great time to dominate that space and gain loyal followers/fans.

Try to think a little bit outside of real estate as well. If you post a picture of a renovation performed by one of your clients use the hashtag #Reno or #KitchenReno. There are a lot of DIY-ers out there who are always on the lookout for renovation ideas. This is a great way to increase the reach of your posts, photos and content to more and more people. How about including #SOLD, #Leased, or #Closing every time you sell or rent a property and post an update of Facebook? Be creative, but simple when using hashtags. Remember, using a weird hashtag that no one will search for doesn't do any good. Search the trends and see what kind of hashtags people are using.

As another example, John uses #MobileMarketing in many posts on his Twitter account, @JohnCoteTV, since it ties in well with his book, *MOBILIZE YOUR CUSTOMERS*. He frequently posts articles that are relevant to mobile marketing in addition to #SocialMediaMarketing and #VideoMarketing among many others. People searching for these topics find his posts and follow him which is one of the reasons he has over 10,000 followers on Twitter.

There are also a number of mobile marketing and social media bloggers who follow John on Twitter and "retweet" his posts. Those retweets share John's Twitter handle and expertise with their entire audience, leading to further engagement. You want to get the Facebook equivalent of a retweet, which is sharing, happening as much as possible. Again, it's not always going to be about real estate. It might be about a social event or commenting on someone's picture or video. Adding hashtags to your Facebook posts can only lead to good things as it widens the audience you are speaking to and increases your chances of getting your posts shared.

John receives the additional benefit of having plenty of content online that prospective clients can follow and read in order to get to know, like and trust him before they do business with him. He is extending that practice into Google+ and Facebook. Additionally, his current clients and people who see him at speaking engagements are giving him reviews on his Fan page that are shared to the reviewer's friends and on John's Fan page, furthering his reach and credibility.

Looking into the future, it's easy to see Facebook allowing promoted hashtag advertising, similar to what Twitter offers. This would allow marketers to implement geo-targeted advertising on relevant hashtagged topics to highly targeted Facebook users.

Embedding videos within your posts

Videos are a very powerful marketing tool. Studies have shown that videos attract more attention than text alone. Video will account for more than 90% of all web traffic by the end of 2013 according to a recent comScore.com study. On Facebook, pictures have the highest interactivity, but video is second. Hubspot.com noted *that On Facebook, videos are shared 12X more than links and text posts combined.* It's hard to argue with that.

But what videos should I post? Videos that are:

- Local, interesting news broadcasts or segments.

- Custom videos created by yourself or your company featuring your listings.

- Video Testimonials from your past or current clients.

- Commercials for upcoming local events that would benefit your audience. Remember - Be the Source.

There are a few ways to use videos within your posts. The first option is by clicking the Photo/Video option, which is the middle of the three options provided. This will only work if you are posting a video that you have recorded or that you have saved on your computer or mobile device. This is not an option for linking or displaying YouTube videos or something interesting you found on Vimeo.com.

The second option is to copy and paste the HTML code allowing you to embed the video within your post. This may sound difficult, but don't sweat it. Sites like YouTube and Vimeo actually WANT you to do this and in turn they make it easy to accomplish. There are many video hosting sites and most of them allow you to embed video. This is how to do it for the most popular two, YouTube and Vimeo.

YouTube - Take any video on YouTube and look below the video and title you will find a few options to choose from: ***About, Share, Add to*** will be spelled out and there may be a few other icons to choose from. The option that we are interested in is the 'Share' option.

Step 1: Click the Share button.

Step 2: Once again you will now notice a few new sub-options to choose from: **Share this Video, Embed, Email**, or **Video call**.

- Click on **Share this Video** to receive the link provided for that video, you may add this link into your post allowing your audience to visit the video's page on YouTube.com.

- Under the link provided in the **Share this Video** section, you will see several logo icons for social media sites. Click on the Facebook logo and this will allow you to share the video on your personal page. Not your Fan page.
  HINT: *You can always post the video on your personal page this way. Next, on the post click **Share**. At the top of the window, click on the drop down menu labeled **Share**: choose **On a Page You Manage**. Then select your business fan page.*

- Click on **Embed** to receive the code to copy and paste into your Facebook post.

- Click **Email** and fill out forms provided to send the video via email.

- Or click **Video call** to display and play the video within a Google + Hangouts chat.

Step 3: To **Embed** the video inside your post simply copy and paste the HTML code provided and past it within your post.

HINT: *Be sure to paste the code after whatever text you are entering into the post. An introduction to the video and why you are posting it is always a good start.*

Vimeo - Go to any video on Vimeo and move your cursor over the video. A small row of icons will appear in the top right corner of the screen: *Like, Later*, and *Share*. Once again, the option that we are interested in is the 'Share' option.

Step 1: Click the Share button.

Step 2: A pop-up window will appear giving you several options, and three of them pertain to Facebook.

- Supplying a link for you to post in your Facebook timeline to allow your audience to visit the video's page on Vimeo.com.

- Under the **Social** section, click on the Facebook logo and this will allow you to share the video on your personal page. Not your Fan page.

- **Embed** - copy and paste HTML code provided into your post to embed the video.
  HINT: *Vimeo goes one step further with embedding videos. Click on + Show Options and you will see that you will be given an opportunity to change the dimensions of the video as well as a few other options.*

Step 3: Click the Share button.

There are many other video hosting sites and most of them allow you to share and embed their videos via social media. It's in their best interest and provides free marketing for their site and service.

Linking to your website

This is where having a website with lots of good content comes into play. I have really been working hard to improve my website, TourHuntsville.com, and create as much high quality content as possible. Good, pertinent, interesting, and reliable content that my viewers can appreciate and use to their benefit. The way my team does this is whenever one of us posts a new blog, resource for buyers or sellers, or a new page on our website we broadcast it on Facebook.

A few months ago I had my assistant write a blog talking about wedding venues and then listing many of the popular venues in our area. This was a huge hit of course with the SERP (search engine results page) on Google for the related search. Many of our Facebook fans really connected with this blog post! A high percentage of women read our blog and that post created quite the conversation. A comment here and another there and before we knew it, we had 40 referral clicks from that Facebook post connecting to our website. The blog can be found here: http://tourhuntsville.com/posts/wedding-venues-huntsville if you would like to read it.

What if I don't have a website?

If you don't have a website with plenty of good content to share with your audience on Facebook, that is okay, too. There are other ways to go about this so do some research. Are there any websites pertaining to your area that have directories of phone numbers, resources and websites for consumers? An event website or your city or county's Chamber of Commerce site will do just fine. Create posts that offer that information to your audience, copy and paste the link in the body of your post and encourage your viewers to check out the site for usual information and resources.

HINT: *Be sure to look closely at which websites you are linking to. Many real estate agents and companies have these types of things on their sites and you definitely wouldn't want to hand over your prospects to these other agents or companies, would you?*

Local and relevant current events or things to do

If everything you post pertains specifically to the real estate industry, folks are going to get bored and tune you out. So, writing about local and current events is a great way to add content, relevance and diversity to your page. And, in my opinion, it is also the easiest. Truly. Stop and think about what you would want to know about your city if you were new to town. Start with one good idea and you'll find that it sparks 5 or 6 more.

EXERCISE: Try it right now. Break it down into categories... let's start with food. Who makes the best pizza in town? This is a great opportunity for you to promote local businesses – stay away from chain restaurants, if possible. Think about locally owned pizzerias and write a short blog post about your favorite spot. What about BBQ? Here in the south, we have a plethora to choose from. Write a short blog about your favorite BBQ restaurant and then pose a question on your Facebook page to generate conversation and interaction. Something like, "Do you like vinegar based or sweet sauces?" Or "Who rules the BBQ Kingdom: St. Louis or Memphis?"

Sports. Again, we Southerners are all about our college teams! Where do you like to go to watch the big game? Who makes the best wings in town? What about drink specials? $1.00 Drafts? Focus on becoming the best possible resource for FUN stuff to do in your town! And, remember Golden Rule #4 – always keep it positive.

Romance. I once wrote a blog suggesting date night ideas the week before Valentine's Day. I polled the women in my life and we came up with three great options for different tastes and budgets that were timely and helpful. Feel free to steal that idea! How about the perfect place to propose? Wedding venues? Best place to watch the sunset with your sweetie?

Farmers Markets. Scope out the best Farmer's Markets in town and share the times and locations. One of our local churches started hosting a summer farmers market in their parking lot every Thursday afternoon. How cool is that? So, we wrote a blog to help spread the word. That one post was <u>shared</u> more than 63 times in less than 4 hours. Notice I said 'shared' and not just 'liked'. That is a huge difference. If your Facebook friends actually like something enough to share it on their page, you've hit a home run!

Entertainment. What about art exhibits or gallery strolls? Museums? Does your town have an active music scene? Our city hosts Concerts in the Park all summer long. We wrote a blog about it and included a schedule the week before the concerts began. Again, that blog spread like wildfire on Facebook.

You see where I'm going with this, right? You should never lack for something to write about. If you do, we provided a vault of 101 posts to help get you started. Remember, be the source!

Financing articles pertaining to mortgages and refinancing

This one is tricky. We all know that, as real estate agents, we have to be careful about quoting rates and offering financial advice. So, ask your mortgage friends for help. I have no doubt that you have a list of 5 or 6 lenders that would love to provide viable, current information about what's happening in their industry. What a great opportunity for your lenders! This is a chance for them to acquire free advertising and you as the agent are becoming an advocate for their business.

Chapter 8

How to use the post scheduler to save you time and energy, spend only 20-30 minutes a week on Facebook and achieve success.

How would you like to take care of most of your posting and status updates on your Facebook Business page in as little as 20-30 minutes once per week? Facebook's post scheduler function allows you to do just that. It's easy to use and scheduling posts to appear whenever you'd like is such a convenience.

Manually posting on Facebook is the way to go hands down. There are plenty of third party companies who offer software that will post for you. Those products are easy to use, very convenient and best of all they work. The problem is that Facebook's algorithm and other quirks make using third-party tools to schedule your posts less than desirable. The Facebook algorithm punishes the production of content from third party sources by giving them a lower EdgeRank score.

As an example, Hubspot.com had always experienced great success with their Facebook marketing campaigns. That is until the day they started to use software to schedule their posts for them. Who wouldn't jump right on an automated posting method? Even if it were a bit costly, wouldn't you want to save your company the time, energy and labor costs to do it manually? Of course you would and keep in mind, they were using their own product.

What Hubspot.com wasn't anticipating was the huge punch in the gut they were about to receive. The number of 'Likes', comments, and engagement they were getting plummeted dramatically. Hubspot.com's team didn't panic, but they had to get to the bottom of the sudden change. After performing a two-week experiment of posting the exact same post manually via the Facebook post scheduler function and not only through their own software product, but also using another comparable product offered by a competitor, the results were obvious. Manually scheduling posts for their

Business page yielded much better results. In fact, they came to this conclusion, "Specifically, we found that content published through third-party API tools suffered 67% fewer likes than content published manually via Facebook.com." They went even further regarding content creation by third parties, "Furthermore, content published through third-party API tools suffered 60% fewer clicks than content published manually via Facebook.com."

Now that you see the benefits of posting content yourself and manually scheduling posts using Facebook.com, let me show you how.

HOW-TO use the post scheduler.

Step 1: Create your post or status update as you usually would. Of course you can attach photos, add links, add YouTube videos, add tags to other pages and events or just include regular text.

Step 2: In the lower-left corner of your post, click on the clock. Then one by one you can add the year, month, day, hour and minute you want the post to be broadcast.

HINT: *Please note that you can only pick the minute at which your post will be scheduled in increments of 10. You can also backdate posts as well.* Language and location targeting is also available while scheduling posts. Click on the *Public* icon and make a choice.

Step 3: Click schedule and now you are finished! It's always a good idea to check on your posts consistently if you do not have automatic notices pushed to your mobile device or tablet. That way you can keep an eye out for comments or any questions you may need to answer. Any comment may be an opportunity for a lead or a referral. Pay attention!

Posting during peak times

According to a study performed by Virtue, a social media management company, the three biggest usage spikes tend to occur on weekdays at 11:00 a.m., 3:00 p.m. and 8:00 p.m. ET. They went more in depth and stated that the biggest spike occurs at 3:00 p.m. ET on weekdays. I have read several other studies and many of them have come to the same conclusion: *Traffic spikes at mid-week from 1pm to 3pm.* That is a good place to start. You also need to track when *YOU* get the best response for *YOUR* updates and post accordingly. There is more information on that in the next chapter on engagement.

Making Facebook part of your routine

A routine is defined as a sequence of actions regularly followed. That is as simple as it gets. Would you consider Facebook to be part of your routine? If so, are you spending your time wisely on Facebook working towards increasing your business? It's easy to get caught up in looking at personal posts and amusing videos. Don't do it. Focus on promoting the business during this time. It's your time; spend it wisely and save the personal stuff for later.

To achieve great results, your must show perseverance and become habitual in your pursuit of success. What a powerful statement. Who said that? Me. I have been telling myself this for years and trying my very best to live by it. To me, this simply means, don't give up and maintain good habits. To succeed and achieve great results for your business using Facebook, you need to add it to your day. Allow marketing your business on Facebook to become habitual and more importantly stay persistent towards creating quality content and actively engaging your audience.

Encourage your advocates to use your post scheduler

Anyone logged in as an administrator on your account can use the post scheduler function. Encourage your advocates that you have appointed as admins to help out as well. Back in chapter 6, I spoke about delegating posting duties amongst your advocates and encouraging them to contribute. The post scheduler can speed up this process and simplify their efforts.

Now you can see how much time and energy the post scheduler tool can save you. Remember the peak times and days and focus on posting during those periods. Maximize your visibility and reach by working smarter, not harder. When done correctly and as part of your routine, 20-30 minutes a week using the post scheduler will be a huge asset to your Facebook marketing campaign. As a reminder, you can use post-scheduling software but it does lower the engagement level of your posts.

Chapter 9

Engaging your fans.

Engaging your fans and followers is THE most important aspect of marketing your business on Facebook. Subsequently, it is also the hardest. How do you capture the attention of your audience? How do you keep it? We provided a chapter with 101 posts to help get your started and here are a few other ideas to kick things off:

- Give your audience something of perceived value – free reports, lists and articles specific to your area.

- Give away something that has a monetary value like a gift card.

- Ask for advice and opinions! People love to interject their opinion especially about decorating, renovations, and their favorite neighborhoods.

- Run contests or surveys on your Facebook business page and make it competitive. Examples might be guessing how much the quote is to do a kitchen renovation on a listing you have on the market. This provides HUGE exposure for your seller's home. Another idea is to quiz your audience on the average sales price of homes sold in a very popular neighborhood in town.

Remember that your Facebook contests don't always have to be related to real estate. For instance, our market happens to be full of engineers and PhD's, many of whom are science fiction buffs. My business partner ran a series of Facebook contests that she entitled 'Nerd Trivia", embedding classic sci-fi trivia questions into QR codes and posting them on Facebook. Her clients loved it! The contest kept them engaged and even inspired some new friends and followers.

Your goal is to eventually get a couple of those people to contact you, turn them into leads and eventually have them purchase or sell homes with you. Let's talk about how I accomplish that consistently and with minimal effort.

Engagement

Likes are important, however they mean nothing if no one is sharing, liking or commenting on your posts. The most important number on Facebook as a marketer is *789 People Talking About This*. Divide that number by the number of people who like the page and you will get a decent idea of what kind of engagement you are getting. Most pages rarely get above 1%; the best pages consistently get well over 20%.

If you want to really *crush* it on Facebook or any social media platform for that matter you have to get creative with your posts to encourage engagement. This is how you get people to stay connected to you. If you're doing the same thing as every other agent in your area, it's very difficult to break out from the crowd and explain to people why they should be doing business with you as a buyer's or seller's agent. Let's face it, there's no shortage of real estate agents and brokers. With the economy turning around, there will likely be an increase of new people coming into the industry. Posting once a week that you have an open house this weekend is *not* going to attract the attention of hardly anyone; there are open houses every weekend!

As a general rule, pictures get more attention than plain text posts or even videos on Facebook. Your mileage may vary so track your posts and see what is working best. In some niches, videos rank higher. We will continue to track this as the global trend is for video to continue to grow in popularity on Facebook, particularly since Vine and Instagram have made it super easy to share short videos quickly. It doesn't have to be a picture of a house. You can place images of cute kids, art, dogs, cats, sunsets in your area, events, cool landscapes or whatever people are interested in. If you only post about your listings, people who are not ready to buy will get tired and may unfriend or stop following you. You don't want to be that person online who is annoying everyone with a constant stream of "buy my stuff" posts.

Another thing you need to test and track is the best time to post. Do a search online for that topic and you will find tons of articles telling you when the best time to post is. The problem is, none of those people tested on YOUR fans. Go into your analytics, *Facebook Insights*, and take a look for yourself. You will be able to figure out very quickly which times tend to get the best response. We suggest you try at 7-9am, 10:30am, 12-1pm, 3pm, 6pm, 8-10pm. These tend to be the times of the day people are checking their accounts since they coincide with waking up, coffee break, lunch, coffee break, after work and after dinner leisure time. Do not post at each of those times on the same day! 1-2 posts per day are usually enough, we don't suggest going more than 4-5 in a day.

We are not suggesting you sit around and waste time on Facebook for half the day trying to be creative. I have outlined how I handle posts and it's easy to do a great job in a short period of time. That's one of the reasons we gave you a list of 101 posts to get you started. Another method to get people sharing and connecting with your posts is through the use of *hashtags*, which I described, in an earlier chapter. Most of the major social media sites have integrated them so you should use them there as well.

Other Social Media platforms to integrate in Facebook tabs

We recommend you install tabs on your business page for all of your active social media sites and see how well they work in driving traffic for you. You are probably not using all of these sites so do not create tabs for social media sites where you are not active, it defeats the purpose. It's very easy to install these using a variety of free services like Woobox, Involver and Heyo. There are many others, just do a Google search. Refer back to Chapter 4 to review your options and how-to's on creating custom tabs and tiles.

YouTube integration should be first on your list since video is such a huge part of what people are typically searching for online. In addition to offering all of your videos in a Facebook tab, you can post your YouTube videos in your timeline as well.

HINT: *You will want to keep them less than 3 minutes long, as those tend to get more views.*

If you are uploading a bunch of videos at the same time, don't post them all to your timeline right away. Set up a campaign that posts one a day for a week or however long it takes to post them. Review Chapter 8 where we covered using the post scheduler. You can also post a link to your YouTube channel or a specific playlist. Channels now have the ability to play a short trailer for new viewers to try and turn them into subscribers. You must do this! It takes just a couple of minutes to shoot a video on your phone and upload it to YouTube. Of course you can do something cool and creative but the important thing is to act and get it done.

Twitter is a bit different in that the frequency of posting does not match up with your fans expectations on Facebook. People on Twitter post a dozen or more times daily. Do not connect your Twitter feed to your Facebook timeline; you will really tick off your fans! They don't want 140 character posts pinging their timeline all day. If they do want that, they will follow you on Twitter or they can click on your Twitter tab in your fan page.

While considering all of the major platforms, understand that several new social media platforms have sprung to the forefront recently. Pinterest has a large following of about 50 million and their demographic skews female, although that is starting to even out. If you are not familiar with Pinterest go to their website and view some of the profiles. They are similar to digital pin boards where people post and tag pictures they find interesting into groups. That sounds like a perfect opportunity to group pictures of your listings or homes in a particular subdivision and name the pinboard after your city and subdivision. As with the rest of the social media sites, you can create a tab inside your Fan page that shows the content in your Pinterest profile.

As we were getting ready to publish this book, video on Instagram was announced. For those who are unaware, Facebook bought Instagram, the rapidly growing picture sharing service, in

2012. They have over 100 million users as we write this. Their service allows you to put different types of image filters on your pictures to make them look worn, old fashioned, sepia toned, black and white, etc and then share them with your friends and family. As a social media service, it's easy to use for promoting yourself and your listings. According to SimplyMeasured.com, as of May 2013, 67% of the top brands in the world are using Instagram. Most real estate professionals have barely scratched the surface of what is possible or are not even aware that it exists.

Instagram is highly mobile optimized and with the addition of 15-second videos, you have a fantastic opportunity to stand out. You can use this to your advantage to create short interesting videos that cater to people looking to buy or sell real estate in your area. You can easily place a tab in Facebook that allows those pictures and videos to be shared from within Facebook both online and via mobile app. The videos can be recorded with your Smartphone. By the way, if you don't have a Smartphone, get one, you'll need it to implement these strategies and tactics!

Here are a few other ideas on how to use Instagram. Put your images together into a slideshow. It's easy to use Keynote or PowerPoint to create a few slides that have pictures of the house in an animated slide show to add more interest to your listings. Create videos of local events showing people from out of town things to do. Encourage followers to submit their own videos and pictures of what they find interesting to do around town. Run contests in Facebook that give people a chance to vote on or like the best images or videos. Instagram has Likes and hashtags as well, give your followers a reason to use them!

There are plenty of cool filters in Instagram, use them to take unique shots of specific details of the house that are interesting and enticing. Then post and share them with your followers. As you post these on Instagram and other social media sites then share them on Facebook, you are creating multiple opportunities for people to share your posts.

Instagram's video service is a direct competitor to Vine, which was purchased by Twitter in 2012. Vine is like Twitter for video. You can upload a video of 6 seconds in length and it's looped so it plays continuously. Many creative people have taken to using it for a variety of funny and interesting (albeit very short) videos. If you choose to use it, you can post those videos into a Facebook tab as well. Since it's such a new service, few Realtors are actually using it at this point. That will give you an advantage so just try it out and see if it's a good fit for your business. It's fast and easy to do. If it lands you a couple of listing or sells one house then it's obviously well worth it.

HINT: *Download the Instagram app on your smart phone, this makes using the new video function quick and easy.*

According to Mashable.com, a leading technology and social media blog, more than twice as many Fortune 100 companies are using Instagram video compared with Vine video even though Instagram just started offering video in June 2013. As with everything in social media, this will change as new entrants emerge and existing players discover new ways to engage people. You can stay on the leading edge of these developments by subscribing to our weekly online broadcast at **SocialMarketingTV.com** where we discuss trends, teach you new techniques that are working in the real world. We will also have interviews of industry leading agents, brokers and social media experts to keep you up to date on the latest developments to improve your revenue.

Contests

We have mentioned contests throughout the book and they are a great way to engage your fans. This is the perfect opportunity to build your list. Facebook owns your fan page and can shut it down anytime so you really need to be getting your followers onto your email or text message list as a backup. When you run your contest ask them for their first name and email. Keep it very simple. You can get a free account on MailChimp to run a small email list with a limited number of emails and subscribers per month.

By the way, DO NOT run your email list from your personal or business email account. That includes Gmail, Yahoo Mail, Hotmail, etc. The CAN SPAM laws require that you have opt out links in every email along with other rules and it's too easy to mess it up. You can get an account for free as mentioned for $20 month to start at most of the major providers (iContact, Aweber, Constant Contact, etc.) All of them provide video tutorials on how to set up email auto-responders. This is an easy way to follow up with people and you own the list forever.

Facebook is very specific in their Terms of Service (TOS) that you must use a third party app to run a contest. As an example, we see this violation all the time on Facebook; asking for "likes" or "shares" of comments or images to enter a contest. Don't do it, it's against the TOS! That can get your page banned. Another no-no is notifying winners on the timeline. That is a very common mistake; we see all kinds of businesses putting pictures of the winners on their timeline.

Another thing to consider is the prize itself. Running a contest for a free iPad will get you a lot of entries, but everyone wants an iPad. Are you actually getting quality leads to enter the contest? Offering prizes that are related to your industry will deliver better results for you. As an example, how about giving away Home Depot gift cards, free gutter cleaning, carpet cleaning, garage organizer shelving, lawn care for a month and so on. The idea is to do giveaways that appeal to homeowners. If you have a decent following, create a survey that asks your followers which of these 3-5 prizes they would like.

Check out some of the sites that offer Facebook contest apps and see what they have to offer. They all have plenty of options for running fun and engaging contests that look great and are easy to implement. Using third party apps will ensure you are staying within Facebook's rules so don't create your own contest. Try some of them and see what works best for you, but don't wait, take action now!

Coupons

Everyone loves a deal and coupons are an easy way to get attention. You can always ask some local businesses if they would be interested in having their coupons on your Fan page as prizes for contests or just to promote themselves on your page. You can cross promote with a sign in their store or on their Facebook page that this offer is available on your Fan page. This is a win-win-win and Facebook users interact well with enticing coupon offers. They frequently share the best coupons with friends and that helps boost your engagement numbers as well.

Extensive research has shown that dollar amount discounts will draw almost twice as many people as percentage discount deals. Fans definitely prefer a dollar amount, even if it's a small number. There are numerous apps you can use for free or small fee like Woobox and others we have mentioned. You can also use Facebook's native app here Facebook.com/coupons.tab

Graph Search

Status updates are the best way to connect with your fans for free, convert some of them into clients and grow your business. Graph Search went live on Facebook just before we published the book and its importance cannot be overstated. Status updates will be part of the Graph Search algorithm and will help you get more traffic. Basically, Facebook will reward you for making comments or posting images and videos that people share. The mobile version is not yet available but it will be soon once they complete testing.

Graph Search is turning Facebook into an online search engine. In that regard, "Likes" are very important because these search results will be based in part on the number of Fans you have. Forbes, TechCrunch and many other high profile media outlets have written articles about why this is important. It allows the user to perform highly targeted searches for things their friends and family have "liked" such as local businesses, images of friends, TV shows they are interested in, videos etc.

HINT: *Be sure to review your privacy settings on your personal accounts. There is a bit of controversy surrounding possible breach of privacy by making their entire Facebook page's content searchable. Facebook staff encourages individuals to pay close attention to privacy settings to ensure there are no issues.*

Not only have they introduced Graph Search, the timeline interface is being updated as well. Although they update features frequently, this particular change will help small business owners grow their pages and fan base faster. One of the new features is the ability to get your ad on the Fan page of your biggest competitor. They are currently testing these features in Australia and New

Zealand, we will post updates on our Fan page when the changes go global.

Facebook is also testing ranked comments to boost engagement according to Mashable.com. This is yet another free traffic source that will help distribute your message to more people, leading to more likes and higher engagement. All of these changes are geared toward helping Facebook provide better content for their users. When you post an interesting status update and it gets comments, likes and shares Facebook's algorithm views this in a positive light and will reward you by showing it to more people. The more traffic you get, the more Fans you get. More fans mean better results in Search Graph and that leads to more traffic.

Facebook recommends some basic things you can do to optimize your Fan page to help you get discovered with these changes. This is very important because this information will appear in Facebook searches. If your information is inaccurate, you will not show up in relevant searches. Make sure your "About" page is completely filled in with your Page name, Facebook "Vanity" URL, (you do have a custom domain name for your Fan page, right?) address, phone numbers, points of contact, hours, appropriate keywords in your description, description of your business, etc. Review Chapter 2 if you have any questions regarding how to update the About section.

Client Reviews and Reputation Management

Another fantastic way to connect with people is to get reviews posted on your Fan page. This is the ultimate engagement strategy since your satisfied clients are telling the community how great you are. You are creating *digital word of mouth advertising*, which is extremely powerful. As an example, John uses an app that allows his clients, readers of his book or people who have heard him speak at an event to leave a review and a rating on a 5 star scale on Facebook. This is done with an easy to install app that appears as one of his Fan page tabs. We installed it on our fan page as well; you can see it and leave a review by clicking here.

In addition to showing up in the tab, the review gets posted on this Fan page timeline on his Fan page timeline and the reviewers timeline as well, which some of their friends will see and can

93

comment on. You can even embed several of the most recent reviews as a Facebook social plugin for your website or blog. Clicking on a review will take them to your Fan page and the rest of the reviews. Whenever someone leaves a review, John always "likes" and comments on it with a thank you post. That helps drive more interaction as well.

You should always follow up with your clients after the closing to get feedback on how things went. The best way to get a review is to simply ASK, like we just did! Your clients will be very happy after successfully closing the sale so ask them at the closing if you can email them a link to review you. I prefer not to ask them to write it while we are standing there together, this allows them more freedom to give an honest opinion and that is what you want. Just be sure to follow up, several times if needed, to get the review. That's why you have email auto-responders. One last thing, it's not ethical to ask for only a good review. There are a variety of questions you can ask to get it done ethically. We tend to ask questions that are worded like this, "Please tell us what you loved about your experience working with your company name?"

Getting the review out in front of the world and beyond your website is very important. It can be a review on Facebook where they post it to your fan page or by posting it in an app as just described. Other social media review sites are very important as well like Google+ Local, Zillow or Yahoo Local. There are plenty of websites for your clients to review you so we encourage you to get them in as many places as possible. Your objective is to have dozens of reviews all over the place to provide third party verification of how awesome you are to potential clients.

With a little extra work, you can record audio or video testimonials from your clients and post them on your website, blog or social media. You will want to get a release form signed to cover yourself; consult your attorney about that. Those types of reviews are very effective and we encourage their use. There is a great, real life example of an HVAC company in Idaho that has over one thousand audio testimonials from satisfied customers on their website! A company employee calls the homeowners for a phone survey 20 minutes after the installation is complete and most agree to be recorded. The reviews are indexed by ZIP code so prospects can listen to people in their own neighborhood. They are DOMINATING their marketplace even though they are more expensive than just about every other contractor in the area due to the high standard of service they provide. By doing the follow up this way, they also get the benefit of quality control to ensure that the sales staff and technicians are doing their jobs correctly.

Imagine for a moment what your business would be like if you had even a fraction of that number of reviews online. If your competitors have a couple of reviews or even 20 reviews and you have hundreds of glowing reviews posted everywhere, who do you think stands a better chance of standing out? This is all part of your reputation management and that is a whole other book unto itself. John actually wrote an extensive chapter about it in his book, *MOBILIZE YOUR CUSTOMERS*. There are plenty of services available to track your online reviews for a fee. You can also set up a free Google Alerts account to track any mentions about your company, brand or name. We will cover this topic in more detail inside of our membership site if there is enough interest.

Chapter 10

101 great posts and status updates to drive engagement.

This chapter will help you get a head start on creating posts that attract attention and capture your audience. Also, many of these post and status update ideas will include an example CALL TO ACTION. Feel free to use each and every one of the post ideas below on your page and don't be afraid to add your own spin to it and make it more personal to you.

Another thing I strongly encourage you to consider when using these ideas, or creating quality posts of your own, is posting this information on your website. Many of these ideas would be valuable content for your website to help your search engine optimization and attract visitors. Kill two birds with one stone and use the content in two places at once. Before you know it, you will have dozens of blog posts and buyer resources on your Facebook page. That will also help your website become a destination. Additionally, you can use them for other social media sites as well.

Great blogging ideas that will intrigue and engage your audience

Hottest new developments in your area

Is new construction hopping in your area? If so, write a short 'review' on the most popular new neighborhood/development and why it's so hot. Make sure you write it from your professional perspective as a real estate agent or broker. This provides a great opportunity to share proprietary statistics from MLS and show off your 'mad real estate skills.'

CALL TO ACTION: What's your favorite new development in town?

Beefing up your home's curb appeal

Explain why curb appeal is so vital in home sales -- first impressions matter! Talk about how important it is for sellers to look at their home with 'fresh eyes', as if they are seeing it for the first time from a buyer's perspective. Suggest that they drive around their neighborhood/town and look for homes that appeal to them. Why? Well, how can they implement some of those details into their existing home? Suggest that you would be happy to visit with them and give them your professional opinion about the most cost-effective ways to enhance their home.

CALL TO ACTION: Pose a question to your readers... "What cost-effective tricks do you have up your sleeve to increase curb appeal?"

Classic Historic color combinations for the exterior of your home

There's a reason they are called 'classics'. When preparing to paint your home, the options are truly overwhelming. One way to 'play it safe' with an exterior paint color choice is to stick with the tried and true. Historic paint colors are timeless. You can also suggest that your readers drive around town and see what appeals to them. Invite them to contact you for a professional opinion. (See a running theme, here?)

CALL TO ACTION: Call me today for a free consultation.

Victorian Architecture and house plans

Many buyers dream of living in and/or restoring a lovely Victorian gem. Empower your readers to dream of their perfect home. Search for and link to some gorgeous Victorian house plans in several sizes. Remember that your readers come in all shapes, sizes, and price points. Start with something affordable, like 1500-2000sq ft. and work your way up to a mac-daddy Victorian mansion. Who knows? You may inspire someone that can actually afford an enormous historic jewel!

CALL TO ACTION: Do you have a favorite local historic home? OR, I can help you build your dream! Call me today for information about local builders, lots and construction financing.

Craftsman home plans and trends

Craftsman style homes are hot! With regard to home plan searches, the word 'Craftsman' is Googled twice as often as any other architectural style. These beautiful homes evoke a sense of timelessness and stability. You have several options here. Research and share information about the origins of the Craftsman style home. Talk about the Sears home kits from the early 1900's that allowed families to build a craftsman home from a kit for $1,920. Your readers will be intrigued and inspired! OR, find and link fantastic Craftsman plans in various sizes as we suggested in the previous paragraph.

CALL TO ACTION: Ask your readers to browse the home plan sites and find some amazing plans to share. Suggest that they specifically look for home plans with spacious, inviting front porches.

What is a termite bond?

We've all heard horror stories about termite infestation and the catastrophic destruction this little winged menace can wreak. Educate your readers on the importance of acquiring and maintaining a termite bond to protect their investment. Be sure you link to and/or reference information from actual termite companies. You don't want to misrepresent yourself as an expert. Be the source! Refer them to a list of local termite/pest companies posted on your website.

CALL TO ACTION: Ask your readers to share information about their favorite local pest control companies. NOTE: Remember our Golden Rule – Be Positive! This topic could inspire people to share horror stories or rant about a local company. Watch for that and edit or delete any negative comments. Reference the section about managing your FB page and protecting your brand.

Why have a home inspection?

We are all afraid of the unknown. Our state of Alabama is the last remaining Caveat Emptor state in the nation. That's Latin for 'BUYER BEWARE!' Scary stuff! Even if you are not practicing Real Estate in Alabama, a home inspection is crucial. A licensed home inspector is trained to spot problems that the average human would never notice, and to make note of 'red flag' issues that could become a problem in the future.

CALL TO ACTION: Ask your readers to brag about and refer their favorite home inspector. Again, watch out for horror stories and/or rants with this one.

What is a home warranty?

You would be surprised how many of our buyers and sellers have never heard of a home warranty. Surprising since they've been around for a very long time! In 1994, a home warranty saved my family roughly $9,000 by replacing two full HVAC systems that were struck by lightning. Most home warranty policies will replace any appliances that cannot be repaired. Be sure to educate yourself on the different companies and their policies. They are all different. Some require an additional rider for HVAC systems and swimming pools. Be sure to quote (and link) to Home Warranty companies and do not presume to be the expert on what is covered and what is not. Tread lightly here.

CALL TO ACTION: Again, ask your readers to relay instances where their home warranty saved them a bundle! And ask which company do they recommend or have had good experiences with.

Edify, Edify, Edify!

Promote local businesses! Your positive restaurant reviews can fall into this category. This is also a good opportunity to promote local tourism attractions and venues. Use discretion when promoting local businesses & tradesmen. Make sure that you are speaking from personal experience. Do not promote someone based on hearsay. By doing this, you are banking your reputation on their services. Also, be certain you comply with your local real estate laws. In our market, we must be careful not to 'steer' clients toward any particular mortgage lender or home inspector. So, I always provide my clients with a list of 3 or 4 reputable companies/agents. It's probably wise to follow a similar practice with your FB posts.

CALL TO ACTION: Engage your audience by asking for their opinion on the Best Of... People love to share their opinions, so give them a chance to!

Contests, Surveys & Conversation Starters

These posts don't require a call to action since they are, by their very nature, inspiring interaction.

Gardening Photo Contest

Run a photo contest and invite your readers to share photos of their favorite plants and perennials. Gardeners love to show off their efforts! A great summertime contest could be to ask them to take a photo of the ugliest homegrown tomato, or a broader category – giant vegetables! Feel free to recruit a local nursery or garden store to judge the photos. You're giving the nursery free advertising; so ask them to provide a gift card for the winner. TAG the garden center and/or the owner to let his/her friends see your post.

DIY Success Stories

Invite people to post their latest DIY projects. Allow your readers to vote and award the winner with a gift card to the local hardware store. Or invite a local interior designer to team with you on this contest and donate a 1-hour consultation to the winner. TAG the interior designer to increase your visibility.

Restaurant Reviews

Create an opportunity for your readers to play food critic. Set a positive tone by saying something about promoting great businesses in your local area. Ask them to tell you who builds the best burger, or which pizza restaurant makes the best pie. Be sure you pay attention to the interactions and edit and/or delete any negative comments. Protect Your Brand.

Adding outdoor living spaces to your home

This is another great opportunity to run a summer contest. Team up with an outdoor living/hardscape business and allow them to judge the photos and award the winner a gift certificate to their store. Be sure to TAG that vendor.

Recipe Contests

Remember, your Facebook page does not have to stick to real estate. Keep it timely, and run a recipe contest in the fall for the best "Game Day Chili Recipe" or "Best Game Day Snack." Post the winning recipe on your website with a link from Facebook.

Real Estate Specific

Buying rental properties

Create and give away a free report, "5 things to consider when you are investing in rental property." This will show you know what you are talking about and it reminds your readers that you are the person to call when it is time to invest.

CALL TO ACTION: Call me today and we can go look at some potential investments! Be sure to provide your contact information.

Investing in real estate

It's easy to talk about something you are passionate about. Sell your product! Write a quick paragraph or two explaining why investing in real estate correctly is a great idea and can yield much higher returns than your average 401k.

CALL TO ACTION: Has your 401k been losing money? Have you ever talked to your financial advisor about investing in rental property instead?

Why buy foreclosures?

Write a short article about the benefits of buying a foreclosure: possible instant equity, buying under market value, potential rental income, etc. This can spark an interest for one of your viewers and open the door to conversations about buying a home. Go get 'em!

Be careful when purchasing a foreclosure property

Inform your audience of what to watch for. Be the source! This is a chance to establish yourself an as expert. Does the property have a right of redemption date? What is a right of redemption date? What inspections should a buyer have performed? What exactly do they mean by 'As Is, Where Is'?

CALL TO ACTION: Let an expert assist you and ensure you make wise decisions. I'm here to help and I would be honored. Call me today and let's get started - (Your) phone-number.

Top 10 reasons to work with a licensed real estate professional

Make this list according to your experiences. Also, if you are a member of NAR, you have access to an abundance of material on this subject. Or, just Google the phrase above! Find a list that works well for you, personalize it (if possible) and post it on your Facebook page. NOTE: Be sure to credit the sources if you do not create your own list. Remember that it's always good to edify others – this does not diminish your professional credibility in any way.

Fair Housing laws for rental property

Share the link to Fair Housing's website (listed below), and encourage any of your audience members who have rental property or that may be considering buying rental property to read it. This pertains to them too.

HUD Fair Housing Site:

```
http://portal.hud.gov/hudportal/HUD?src=/progr
am_offices/fair_housing_equal_opp/FHLaws/yourr
ights
```

CALL TO ACTION: Can anyone list the different classifications that the Fair Housing Act protects?

Sex Offender Registry

This is a tough one. As real estate professionals, we cannot steer buyers toward or away from any area. However, we can educate our clients and Facebook audience about the laws pertaining to sex offenders, and link to the resources that they need to make an informed decision. The Sex Offender Registry is a public record. Find the resource for your area and provide a link on your website. Write a brief paragraph about the importance of checking the sex offender registry when buying, selling or renting real estate.

Creating Home Searches and linking to your website

Log on to your website, not as an administrator or webmaster, but as a consumer. Conduct a home search and find results pages that would be popular to many of your viewers. Copy and paste the exact URL and paste this as a link in your post. Viewers who click on this link will now be actively searching for homes on your website! Isn't that the goal here? For example, your URL might look like this:

```
http://tourhuntsville.com/idx/?idx-q-
PropertyTypes%3C0%3E=2960&idx-q-
PropertyTypes%3C1%3E=2956&idx-q-
PriceMin=150001&idx-q-PriceMax=200000
```

CALL TO ACTION: What criteria are you looking for in a home? Shoot me a message and I'll send you a custom search.

Decoding Real Estate

What the heck is PPSQFT? The real estate industry is full of acronyms and strange industry specific terms. Here's a topic that you can address with authority. Start by decoding the popular acronyms: PPSQFT, DOM, HOA, Cntrl2. Later, unearth your old real estate school handbook and run through the glossary. Find obscure real estate terms and teach your readers about 'functional obsolescence' and 'ad valorem real estate taxes.'

Fastest selling price point in your area

This is another opportunity to show off your skills and enthusiasm for your market. Pull sold stats from your MLS system and dazzle your readers with actual data. Keep it generic! Too many numbers and details may injure their brains and/or cause them to tune you out.

Home Related Topics & Tips

Safety tips for baby-proofing your home

This is an easy one to Google. I have no doubt that at least 50 parenting sites provide a list. Go through and gather the top 5 or 10 and make your own list or link to their list and credit them. The call to action will generate a lot of response, as this is always an interesting and timely topic for new moms.

CALL TO ACTION: What tips can you share to baby-proof your home that you have used?

Home Owners' Associations – Know Your Rights and Responsibilities

This is a hot topic in our area and can be a hotbed of controversy! Volunteers run most HOA's with little or no professional oversight. Consequently, there are organizations and websites dedicated to this subject. See if you can find your local resource and share their contact information. Again, watch for negative feedback and/or rants.

Top 5 Ways to Lower Your Power Bill

I'll bet your local utility provider has something like this on their website. But it should be easy to Google and compile your own list from various national websites, as well. Be the source!

CALL TO ACTION: What tips and secrets can you share to keep your power bill low?

Blown Insulation vs. Old-School Batting

This is another hot topic in our area. Several of my home inspector friends hate when blown insulation is applied to the inside of a roof because it can mask leaks and make them virtually undetectable until a small problem becomes a catastrophe. Poll your contacts in the industry and provide information on the latest products.

CALL TO ACTION: Ask your readers to share their thoughts and experiences.

Composite Siding vs. Aluminum Siding

Provide information about both products and the cost differences. Interview and quote a local builder about which product he/she prefers. This gives you an opportunity to do that magical thing that brings us joy and high-visibility. TAG that builder! This allows all of his Facebook friends to see that you are edifying him.

HINT: Remember to tag the builder *Using Facebook As* your personal account. Do this by commenting on the post and tag the builder there. This will accomplish the same thing.

Building for Baby Boomers – Aging in Place

This is a really hot topic in the building industry right now. Because of the Baby Boom of the 1950s and 1960s, a large percentage of our population is reaching the stage in life where mobility is an issue. First floor master suites, hands-free plumbing fixtures and levered (arthritis friendly) door handles – these are just some of the things that are appealing to our buyer's over 60. Another great opportunity to interview, quote and TAG a local builder.

CALL TO ACTION: What extras or features would you like to see more builders use when building homes for retirement?

Making Your Home Handicap Accessible

Similar topic to the Baby Boomer post, but this topic encompasses folks of all ages with mobility issues. Fair Housing may provide some great information about this one. This is also a great opportunity for you to run a search in your MLS to see how many homes are listed as handicap accessible. I think you may be shocked to see how few there are. Do any of your local home builders specialize in handicap conversions and modifications? Be the source!

CALL TO ACTION: Do you think that all homes should be built handicap friendly to prepare for the future?

What is a Load-Bearing Wall?

Okay, unless you happen to have a home builder's license, don't try to explain this one on your own. Again, interview, quote and TAG a local builder. Or Google the subject and compile the data then write your own blog post. Be sure to cite your sources and do not portray yourself as an expert.

Protecting Your Investment – Top 10 Easy Home Maintenance Habits

Here is another great opportunity to educate your readers. Define the term "Deferred Maintenance" then Google something like "Easy Home Maintenance Tips" and see what comes up. Compile a list of 3, 7, 12 or more quick and/or easy ways to keep your home in tip-top shape (i.e. change the dang air filter!)

CALL TO ACTION: Which maintenance issues have come back to bite you over the years? What advice can you share from experience?

How to Keep Your Bathroom Whirlpool Tub Clean and Mildew-free

I love this one! Have you ever seen what's growing in the jets of an unused whirlpool tub? Particularly when said tub is sitting in the master bathroom of an unoccupied listing. Seriously nasty stuff! The very best way to keep the jets clean is to USE the system on a regular basis, but even then, whirlpool jets are a breeding ground for bacteria. Google the title of this post, read, paraphrase and post the best solution.

Creating a Home Fire Safety Plan with Your Family

Great opportunity to be the source and let your readers know that you care about their families! The Internet will provide an enormous amount of information about this subject. Find one that speaks to you and post a link to it. This is one of those instances where you don't want to paraphrase or presume to be an expert. Link to an expert!

Creating a Storm Safety Plan with Your Family

Our area has just been named one of the most Tornado-prone regions of the country, so this is a hot topic in North Alabama. Again, don't try to be the expert here. Google the natural disasters most prevalent in your area, research prevention and preparation then find the best resource available to link to.

Storm Shelter Options for New Construction and Existing Homes

Many home builders are adding storm shelters during construction. Some are located under the floor of the garage; others are using the master bedroom closets. Google the options available in your market and link to the experts. There are also a wide variety of options that can be installed in your existing backyard. Be sure you research the vendors you include! You want to recommend reputable companies whose products meet or exceed required safety standards.

Home security systems

Home security systems are evolving rapidly and the technology involved is becoming super enhanced. There are so many things that a security system can do for you now besides set off an alarm for an intruder. Write a blog post announcing the benefits of having a system to protect their homes and research and compile a list of security companies who operate in your area and share this list in a post with your viewers.

CALL TO ACTION: Do you have a security system? Do you know that for as little as $1.00 a day you could increase the protection of your home? Someone PLEASE share a story with me about when your security system proved its worth. I'd love to hear about it!

Black mold – the dangers and mitigation options

We often fear what we cannot readily see, and black mold absolutely falls under this category. Write a post giving your audience a clue of what to look for when it comes to black mold. Google the subject and there is a plenty of information available from experts all over the Internet.

CALL TO ACTION: Remind your viewers to keep an eye out for black mold, sometimes this is not on the forefront our or minds nor a priority. It should be and it will feel good to be the person who reminds your clients and following of this potentially fatal issue.

Healthy Crawlspaces – how to prevent mold and fungus from invading your home

Mold happens, especially in crawlspaces. Write a post to inform your audience of the top three ways to prevent mold and excessive moisture from entering your crawlspace: Vapor barriers, venting, and sealing the foundation blocks.

CALL TO ACTION: Do you have a crawlspace? Is it protected against mold and moisture? If so, which company did you use or did you do it yourself?

What is Radon?

According to the EPA, radon is a naturally occurring, cancer-causing, radioactive gas, which comes from the breakdown of uranium in soil, rock and water. Obviously, the EPA is a terrific source for this post. They have posted a Citizen's Guide to Radon on their site that is very well done. They even provide an interactive map so that your readers can check to see how prevalent radon is in their area. Educate your readers and link your source.

Radon mitigation techniques and systems

Many areas in our region are high in Radon due to the abundance of mountains and hills. Obviously, radon is dangerous. Don't pretend to be an expert. Google "radon mitigation" in your local area and interview a respected vendor. Link, Friend & TAG!

Doggy doors – installation and safety tips

Dog-lovers abound! I have friends that are more obsessed with their dogs than their children. Actually, anything pertaining to pets is popular on Facebook. There are some really cool new options in the world of doggy doors. Electronic models with motion sensors, screen doggy doors for your patio, weatherproof options, just to name a few. Research and dazzle your readers with all the cool new innovations. Find something particularly new and interesting to lead off with and include photos. Just be sure to give photo credit and link to the vendor sites.

CALL TO ACTION: Has anyone installed one of the new electronic Doggy Doors? How is working?

Green Cleaning for hardwood floors

Steam mops, biodegradable spray cleaners... loads of new products are out there for safely cleaning and preserving the beauty of hardwood floors. Research and share! Be the Source!

Clearing the air – maintaining your HVAC duct work for a healthier environment

How many times has your home inspector discovered clogged, shredded and/or disconnected duct work in one of your local listings? Your readers will be amazed (and probably disgusted) by how filthy the average HVAC duct systems can be. Educate them on the importance and value of having their duct work evaluated and repaired. Interview a reputable air conditioning company, link, friend and TAG!

CALL TO ACTION: Post an inspection picture of a dirty duct in a particular neighborhood to give it a more local feel then ask when was the last time they had their ducts cleaned.

110

Structural/Foundation Repairs

This is a subject that I know a great deal about. Huntsville is located in the western most foothills of the Appalachian Mountains. I actually live on a small mountain (people living in the Rocky Mountains would consider it a hill!) With mountain living comes structural instability, it's just a fact of life. Cracked foundations sound really scary, and repairs can be costly. Research the different types of structural repair options and companies in your area. Educate your readers so that they will be prepared (and hopefully less frightened) if they are ever faced with structural issues in their home. Different areas have different environmental stresses that lead to structural problems, be sure to highlight local issues.

Home insurance riders and options

Everyone needs insurance, and those who buy homes with a mortgage HAVE to have it. Who do you know and trust in the area that sells home owners insurance? Call or email them and ask them to write a quick blog post or article talking about the importance of home owners insurance and how the rates are configured. Also, research and compile a list of the most common riders to home owners insurance policies and tell your audience what they do.

CALL TO ACTION: Ask your viewers to share whom they have their home owners insurance with and what they like about that company. Are you covered if your subdivision "backs up" into your home?

Real Estate Financing

Teaching your audience about financing is a grand opportunity. Make sure they don't just take your word for it, but also keep a list of 3 or 4 lenders handy while posting these below.

How to get pre-qualified to buy a home

What a huge topic! Talk to your mortgage buddies and have them send you a list of requirements to get pre-qualified to buy. What are the minimum credit score and debt-to-income ratios to qualify?

111

Share this list with your viewers, encourage them to take the first step and see if they can become pre-qualified.

How to raise your credit score

There are free reports on how to raise your credit score all over the Internet! Link to these reports or share the how-to within your post. Be sure to give compliments to the source. You couldn't imagine how many times this exact question is searched every day. Many people are looking into this topic, be the provider of the answers.

Mortgage options for first-time home buyers

Once again, call up a few of your mortgage buddies and get them to send you some information about what products they are offering for first time home buyers. Be sure to ask if there are any 100% financing options and what the rates are looking like on that particular day. Post these options with a headline to grab your audience's attention: 100% financing available to first time home buyers, minimum credit score 660. Make sure your headline is appropriate and coincides with the offers you were provided.

What is income to debt ratio?

Write a short post about what income to debt ratio is and the different limits that are required for financing in today's market. There are countless resources online to guide you. Or link to a mortgage company's website that has an article explaining this concept and its importance.

The truth about Reverse Mortgages

As the population ages, thousands of people are retiring every day. Reverse mortgages are becoming popular and can be an asset to many seniors. Talk with mortgage brokers and bankers and find out who in your community specializes in reverse mortgages. Then gather some information about this and post it on your Facebook page. You never know who might be contemplating this for themselves or their parents. Be the source!

Financing Investment Property

Buying an investment property is not the same ball game as buying a home to occupy. There are different rules involved regarding financing, taxes, insurance and protocol. Compile a list of 10 differences or things consumers should be aware of when thinking about investing in property.

The Ins & Outs of Construction Financing

This is a great one to get the attention of your more affluent members of your audience. Building a custom home is typically more common among higher income clients. Research the process of obtaining construction financing and become knowledgeable on the subject, then post your findings.

What is PMI?

Do you know how many people see the acronym PMI in advertisements and online and do not even know what it means? Inform your audience about mortgage insurance and what it actually is. How much does it cost? Why do I need it? Are there any loan products available that don't require mortgage insurance?

Who is Fannie Mae?

Is she someone you know? Write a quick bio on Fannie Mae and post it on your page. Add little tidbits about the forming of Fannie Mae (how old she is) and what exactly she does. Capture your readers as if you are telling them about a real person. For example:

I am 75 years old.

I am female.

I've never been married.

I own over 100,000 homes last time I checked.

I have over 7,200 employees under me.

I produce over 22.9 Billion dollars a year in gross revenue.

Who am I?

See if anyone can guess her name? Make it a contest.

Gardening

Know Your Zone!

The USDA (Department of Agriculture) has divided the United States into 11 growing zones. Basically each zone is 10°F warmer (or colder) in an average winter than the adjacent zone. Plant hardiness is ranked based on this zone. There are dozens of USDA Zone maps available online. Determine your zone, link to a zone map, and suggest a few plants that are well suited to your particular environment. You can also link to local Facebook pages for gardening enthusiasts that have tips and pictures of beautiful landscapes in the local area. Ask some the frequent posters to that page if they will write a short article about the best perennials to plant and/or favorite local vegetables.

CALL TO ACTION: Place a relevant picture of a vegetable or flower and ask what do people enjoy planting and why. What are some of the easiest plants to grow/most drought or heat tolerant?

Flowering Shrubs – Beauty that Comes Back Year After Year

Adding flowering shrubs to your landscape is a great way to improve your curb appeal. Most flowering shrubs are perennial, meaning they go dormant in the winter and come back in the spring, making them a great investment. No need to replant year after year. Research the best varieties of flowering shrub for your area and post photos and links to local nurseries.

CALL TO ACTION: Post a picture of some beautifully landscaped properties in the area and ask others to post their pictures. TAG a photo of a shrub that grows well in your area and see who can identify it, especially if it is not the standard "new subdivision" variety.

Creating a Green Screen – Best Plants to Create Privacy

You would be surprised how many times this topic enters into my real estate conversations with clients. Most buyers are looking for privacy in their backyard. Many times the topography in our area creates a challenge, particularly in developed neighborhoods. And, many developed neighborhoods place limits and restrictions on the resident's fencing options. Plants, however, are generally exempt from these restrictions and can provide a wonderful solution. For instance, there are two options that do particularly well in our area – crepe myrtles and thuga. Crepe myrtles are a terrific choice to create an extension above an existing privacy fence. Thuga is a variety of evergreen that can grow 4-5 feet per year in full sun. Research options in your area and offer SOLUTIONS to backyard privacy issues.

Backyard Birding & Bird-friendly Gardens

According to a popular birding society, there are more than 50 million 'birders' in the United States. Many of those are over the age of 50 (it's those active baby boomers again.) This is one of those topics that might just land your website on page one of Google! It's that popular. So, if possible, make sure you include this blog on your website and link it to Facebook. Research wild backyard birds commonly found in your area and suggest ways to attract them to your yard. CAUTION: Make sure you give credit where it's due. Wild bird photographers take their craft very seriously and copyright infringement is not cool.

Creating a Butterfly Sanctuary in Your Backyard

Everyone loves butterflies! Random fact: Did you know that butterfly tattoos are the most popular choice among women? Certain plants attract butterflies more than most. Research and share the options best suited to your area and climate zone. You can also provide popular butterfly garden designs and/or links to a local nursery.

CALL TO ACTION: Pictures are always a plus. Ask parents to post videos of their kids playing in a butterfly sanctuary at the zoo or botanical gardens. Those types of videos tend to generate a lot of traffic.

Proper Pruning Techniques & Schedules for 5 Popular Trees & Shrubs

Have you ever heard the term 'Crepe Murder'? This is the term used by gardening enthusiasts to describe the improper pruning of the Crepe Myrtle Tree. Technique is important and timing is everything. Pruning should be done at specific times during the growing season. There are tons of pruning videos available on YouTube. Find and link videos featuring trees and shrubs popular in your area. You can even create a series leading up to spring. Remind your readers when it's time to prune and post a video pertaining to a different plant once a week. Be the source!

Home Improvement

Most bang for your buck – Highest value renovation ideas

As real estate agents, we know the answer to this question. Renovated Kitchen? Over the top Master

Bedroom Suite? Updated Bathrooms? What's the biggest bang for my buck? You can Google this subject and find loads of great input from national sources, but every market is different. I would bring it a little closer to home. Call a local Appraiser, preferably someone that you've worked with who is respected in your area, and ask for their opinion. Friend them and TAG them!

CALL TO ACTION: This is a great one, just ask, "What are the top 3 things you should do to make your house perfect!"

Adding a water feature to your home

Are you a plumber or landscape designer? Probably not, so, ask the experts. Your local nursery and hardscape professionals can provide wonderful input here. Friend them and TAG them!

CALL TO ACTION: As before, post pictures and videos of cool water features and ask for more of the same.

116

Feng Shui tips for an inviting home

Tons of great information is available online. Feng Shui has been around for eons and the laws are not affected by trends or location. This is an easy one. Google, gather and link especially to videos that show how well the concept works.

Hottest paint color trends

This was another home run blog for us. My mother was obsessing about paint colors last fall and Googled 'hottest paint colors for 2013'. This sparked a blog post that ended up hitting page one of Google, generating one of the highest organic search responses we've ever received. It was also a huge hit on Facebook and was viewed and shared a record number of times.

Pergolas and Arbors – simple construction ideas to add charm to your home & landscape

Great opportunity to share plans and DIY instructions. There are hundreds available online. Explain how a simple arbor could enhance curb appeal, and how adding a pergola over an existing concrete slab can create an outdoor living space.

10 Easy Kitchen Upgrades

You can make this one local, as well. Visit your favorite kitchen & bath store, or talk to a well-respected remodeling contractor. Better yet... call one of your flipper/builder friends and find out what they do to update the kitchens when they flip a house. Remember to friend and TAG them!

CALL TO ACTION: Has anyone done an "Upgrade in-a-Day" to their kitchen? What was the easiest upgrade they have done?

Converting your swimming pool to salt water

Your favorite pool store can provide information on the costs and benefits associated with saline pool conversions. Link them and TAG them!

CALL TO ACTION: Add pictures of great new pools the local pool company converted and ask people to comment on what they love about salt water pools.

Easy, Low-Cost Irrigation for your Planting Beds

Soaker hoses & drip irrigation systems are cost-effective and easy. Check out a brand call Snip-n-Drip that allows you to easily customize their system to fit your bedding space. You could also talk about rain barrel systems and downspout diverters to easily collect, store and reuse rainwater in your garden. Google Gardener's Supply Company for some terrific options. Link them!

Adding style & character to your patio with decorative concrete

Decorative concrete is a great way to enhance the look of existing patios and walkways. It's a particularly great choice for pool surrounds in that you have the option of adding texture for safety. If you don't know a reputable vendor, call your favorite pool company and ask for a recommendation. Interview them and link to the post. Let the vendor show off their before and after photos. Friend and TAG them! If you have a large enough following, start a contest to win a decorative concrete makeover with the vendor providing the service in exchange for the promotion.

Enclosing a carport – adding value to your home

This is another one of those posts that is going to require expert input from a reputable builder or remodeler. I would also check with your favorite appraiser to get some numbers on the actual 'value added' difference between a carport and a garage. Friend and TAG!

Kitchen counter top trends and options

We all know that a great kitchen remodel can quite literally SELL a house! And granite countertops are one super popular component. So, encourage your readers to do their homework and use their money wisely when embarking on a kitchen project. Explain the various product options (natural stone, engineered, concrete) and link to vendor sites so that they can gain perspective on costs.

118

CALL TO ACTION: People love kitchen makeovers, post some pictures and ask for others to post a picture of their remodels. Ask local contractors to post images of their most recent jobs, just have them keep it informal with no sales pitch.

Antimicrobial Counter Tops for the Home

The Quartz countertop maker Silestone® claims to be the only countertop with built-in Microban® antimicrobial product protection to safely fight the growth of odor-causing bacteria 24/7 for the life of the product. Consequently, antimicrobial surfaces are becoming more and more popular with homeowners. Provide a link to the Silestone® site to explain some of the reported benefits of the product. This could also be a great cost-comparison post. Take some of the numbers from your countertop post and compare the cost of engineered countertops to that of the antimicrobial product.

Cultured Marble is back!

Did you know that many builders are now shying away from installing granite counter tops in 'family' bathrooms and laundry areas? Do you know why? It's primarily due to hair products and teenagers. Many of the hair products used by your average teenager are harmful to natural stone and can cause something similar to hyper-erosion. The same holds true for laundry products. Consequently, cultured marble products have seen a revival in popularity over the past few years. Research, interview and educate your readers on their options. Link and TAG your sources!

Removing popcorn from your ceilings

Smooth ceilings are the standard right now. Many "Do it Yourselfers" are removing the popcorn from the ceilings of older homes by themselves and it is a pain in the rear! Help them out by posting a few great tips to help them in the process. Google "Removing popcorn from your ceilings" and see what you come up with. Share the tips and advice with your audience in a post. Be sure to link to your sources.

CALL TO ACTION: Post some pictures and ask for before and after pictures when they are done with their project.

Painting over existing wood paneling

Textured walls are becoming more popular in recent years. Sometimes, this look can be achieved without over-hauling a room by taking down old paneling and replacing it with drywall, then adding some texturing. You could also simply paint the wood paneling! This can really add some character to any room and give your old world room a much needed face lift. Conserve your energy and funds by reusing existing materials. Write a blog or short post about this and post on your page. Include pictures if you have done this your self, or use pictures from the web.

Adding wainscoting for traditional charm

Elegance can be achieved many times without spending a fortune Add wainscoting to any room to transform the space into something new and classy. There are countless "How To" videos on YouTube.com taking you through the steps, one by one. Link to these videos or embed your favorite "How To" video on the subject to share with your audience. Include a short paragraph above the video in your post explaining how wainscoting can add value to your home and give it an upscale look.

Adding storm windows and doors

Did you know that adding storm windows and doors not only help protect you from storms and heavy rains, but also can help drastically lower your electric bill? Older single pane windows let out a lot of heat in your home in the summer time and cool air in the winter. Protect your utility bill and give your heat pump a break by installing storm windows and doors if your home has single pane windows. *Use this short paragraph in a post and link to a few company's websites that you may know and trust or pick a few that you have heard good things about in your area. Give these to your audience in the post.

Composite Decks vs. Treated Wood Decks

Research the various products available and describe the pros and cons associated with each -- be sure to include anything new and innovative. Your readers love to hear about new products coming on the scene. Be the source! There are several deck construction cost-comparison studies available online. Link the source and provide a synopsis of your findings.

DIY Shade Solutions for Sunny Backyards

Pergolas, sail shades and roll-out products are just a few of the options available out there. Again, look for innovative new products. It's always great to be able to dazzle your readers with something they've not seen before. Otherwise, provide links and cost-comparisons on the various products you find.

Decorating Style Tutorial

List and describe some of the more popular decorating styles -- Art Deco, Arts & Crafts, Transitional, Traditional, French Country, Modern and the list goes on. There are numerous resources online to draw from. As a real estate professional, you are likely in and out of homes on an almost daily basis. What are the most prevalent and popular styles in your area? There are a lot of options for interaction with this one! You could ask your readers to comment on which style they favor, OR show photos of two different rooms/styles and ask your readers to vote on which they like best.

Urban Living Options

Many folks, myself included, love the idea of living in a spacious urban loft. Are there any loft-type properties in your area? If so, this presents an opportunity for you to talk about the benefits of loft living (Google it), and to showcase specific projects and properties. Remember to ask permission if you are featuring someone else's listing, and certainly make sure you are complying with your Real Estate Commissions rules and regulations.

Smart Home Products

Describe and link some of the MANY innovative new products for your home -- maybe the new Nest Thermostat system or robot vacuums. As we've mentioned before, try to find something that your readers have never seen. Ask your readers to share (link) something new that they've discovered.

CALL TO ACTION: Ask for pictures or videos of funny or innovative ways people have used their Roomba.

Ultimate Kid Spaces

How would your daughter or granddaughter like a storybook castle bed? Would your son like to sleep in a pirate ship? Search for photos and articles (particularly DIY) about dream bedrooms for kids. Pinterest is always a great source for things like this. Invite your readers to share photos they've found, or better yet... rooms they've actually created themselves. This could also be a good opportunity to feature great tree houses or over-the-top play sets.

Invisible Fence

There are many articles online comparing the benefits and costs of invisible fence systems. Research and share your findings. If you're going to provide a cost analysis, make sure you link your source. Have a local vendor write an article for you and post it. Ask your readers to share personal experiences and opinions.

Adding Gutters to Your Home

There are loads of options here. You can explain the benefits of adding gutters and/or talk about the various systems available. Gutter guards are a popular option, as are rain barrel systems, which can capture and store the water for use in the garden. Be sure you link to any new and interesting product options.

Local Info & Things to Do

As real estate professionals, it is important to be aware of all the things to do in your community! I'm not saying that an agent in NYC should know everything about all of the attractions in the city, but you should have a good grasp of what entertainment and attractions your area boasts. This is very important when dealing with relocating families or individuals. Property is the product you sell, but the area you serve is your store. Know what else is there besides for sale signs.

Award winning schools in your area

Which schools are award winning in your community? Share these results and statistics with your audience! Research and find out why they are award winning. This will give a good shout out to the school. Be sure to tag the Schools' Facebook pages if they have one.

School zones can make or break a deal

Schools are perhaps the most important factor when finding a new home. It's important even if you don't have kids because poor schools can reflect lower value and tough resale. Link to GreatSchools.org in a post and encourage your audience to check out the scores of schools in their neighborhood. This might spark a move in their future. You be the one to provide this information to them and create the awareness and you're more likely to be the one who helps them into a new home and/or sell their existing one.

CALL TO ACTION: Why did you pick the area where you live? Was the school zoning a factor?

Magnet Schools in your area

Not all cities and areas have magnet schools, but if the communities you serve do, make a list of these schools and link to their websites. Explain to your viewers what a magnet school is just in case someone doesn't know.

CALL TO ACTION: Does your child, or children you know, go to/or have gone to a magnet school? Did they like it? Please share your experiences with me; I'd love to know!

Dance studios

No matter where you are, dance studios are a BIG deal to little girls. Many of your audience members may have children who are in dance or wanting to start. Compile and post a list of dance studios in the communities that you serve as a resource for your followers.

CALL TO ACTION: Do your children or a child you know take dance lessons? Where do they go?

Public pools and summer swim leagues

Not every town or community has public facilities/pools but on the other hand, many do. Post a list of the public pools in your area and link to their websites. Include hours or operation or if the openings are seasonal, add that as well.

City Sports Leagues for Children

"Fall ball is about to start! Did you get kids signed up?" (Great headline idea and provide the link to the registration page.) Periodically throughout the year, post a schedule and links to city recreation websites for your viewers. Recreational sports are a tremendous outlet for children and you should support this!

CALL TO ACTION: Post and ask for images of opening day activities for each of the sports.

Ballroom Dancing Studios in your area

Did you know that dance lessons and ballroom dancing could increase your confidence level and endurance? (Great headline for your post.) Compile a list of dance studios that offer ballroom dancing lessons and post this on your page. Pair this post with a small list of movies that have to do with this genre of expression, i.e. "Dirty Dancing", "Shall We Dance", "Take the Lead", "Assassination Tango", and "Dance With Me"

5 family friendly fun weekend activities in your area

Here is your chance to showcase your community! Make a list of 5 fun and family oriented activities that are in your area and post them on your page. Think outside the box a bit, try to include something that could be a best kept secret or maybe a new place or event that is not too well known as of yet.

CALL TO ACTION: Did I miss a couple? What are your favorite family friendly weekend activities?

Best hiking and biking trails

Attention all outdoors and fitness enthusiasts! (Great headline for your post.) Write a quick blog entry listing some popular hiking trails in your area and include any maps or pictures you can find. Hiking and biking are really popular almost everywhere. This will be a great resource to your audience.

CALL TO ACTION: What is your favorite hiking or biking trail? What do you love about it? Please share, I'd love to know more about these trails! Post a picture and ask people to identify where it was taken.

Dog parks in your area

Are there any dog parks, dog friendly parks or beaches in the communities you serve? Make a list of them and share them in a post on your page. Good to know if you ever have to "puppysit" for a friend. Be sure to share a photo of you guys...or just your dog (if you have one) enjoying the park.

CALL TO ACTION: Where else do you like to take your dog or pets?

Private Schools in your area

Getting a private school education is really important to some families. Research and then compile a list of private schools in the areas you serve and write a short blog about common reasons parents may choose for their children to attend private schools. Google it, there are countless resources and articles out there giving examples and ideas. If you don't want to write a segment about this, simply link to the articles that you have found that are current and relative.

CALL TO ACTION: Can anybody recommend their favorite private school in town? What makes it so great and what advantages do you see for getting a private education?

How to form a neighborhood watch

This is not applicable to everyone, but this is something that many people are passionate about. I've found this how-to article and it's an interesting read. Share this link with your viewers or write your own article if this is a subject that you are knowledgeable about.

http://www.wikihow.com/Form-a-Neighborhood-Watch

5 Great Date Destinations in your area

Romance is always a good subject to talk about. This is another opportunity to showcase some local hot spots or whole in the walls. What this also accomplishes is it shows that you are quite knowledgeable about the areas you serve and this helps establish you as an expert. If you don't know much about romantic restaurants or attractions in town, this is the perfect opportunity to learn.

CALL TO ACTION: What are your favorite date places? Did anything extra special happen to you there? Please share :)

Fitness centers in your area

People are constantly thinking about fitness centers and getting into shape. This doesn't only come into conversation in early January. Compile a list of fitness centers and workout facilities in the communities you serve and post them on your page. This will be a resource for your audience and might be a catalyst for one of your followers to get back into shape and get their butt in gear. You never know when that is just the reminder they needed and maybe years down the road they will thank you for it.

CALL TO ACTION: Can anyone recommend a gym for me to join? I am interested in group fitness classes and Pilates. (If you aren't, simply change the subject of interest to something more appropriate.

That's 101!

We have given you 101 posts to get you started. Now you have the ability to write hundreds more with the ideas we have given you. Once you get into the habit of doing this, it will become second nature and will take very little of your time. You will eventually discover, as I did, that this technique will provide you with excellent engagement, leads and eventually sales.

Chapter 11

Mobilize your marketing to stay connected, Facebook Insights, Protect your brand.

Taking it mobile

Facebook stated that 64% of their traffic is on mobile devices as of June 2013. Obviously, more and more people are experiencing Facebook from their mobile device. That trend is growing rapidly everywhere. Mobile searches will exceed desktop searches by the end of 2013 according to comScore.com. All of your social media and websites need to be optimized for mobile. That means if people need to pinch and zoom to read your website, you need to fix it. Facebook has struggled with their mobile strategy to date and not everything is perfect, but they are continually improving. Instagram was created as a mobile only app originally and that was one of the reasons Facebook bought them. Posting video content is a very important strategy and mobile optimization is critical since 90% of online searches will be for video by 2014. Fortunately, YouTube handles the encoding for mobile devices automatically. The video on Instagram feature we previously detailed also handles the mobile optimization automatically as does Vine of course.

As you create your online marketing strategy, you must consider how you will reach your fans via mobile devices. Consider how they are using their smart phones in their everyday life and determine how you can reach them consistently with valuable and timely content.

Facebook apps for your mobile device or smart phone

Apple recently unveiled the all-time most-downloaded apps and as you can probably guess, Facebook holds the top spot in the free downloads category. "Market Watch", by the New York Times, states that the average user spends a whopping 6 hours and 49 minutes a week on Facebook mobile apps! There are a few other apps offered by Facebook and they all serve a purpose.

Facebook Home is the main app most of you are probably quite familiar with. This app is the gateway in which over a hundred million people stay in touch with loved ones, stalk exes, and announce to the world that they just found $5. I mentioned several times in earlier chapters about making Facebook part of your routine, your audience has already done this. So have many of your competitors. Use mobile to easily stay connected to the conversation if you have not already done so.

Facebook Messenger is really starting to pick up steam! The world has been searching desperately for a newer and more updated version of AIM (AOL Instant Messenger), which dominated the market for one on one messaging for over a decade. Facebook has answered the call, finally! Having access to this mobile app can alleviate the need for texting in many cases and it's free.

Facebook Pages Manager is one to pay attention to. I use this app dozens of times per day and I couldn't maintain my Facebook Business page as well without it. The main benefit of having this app as well as Facebook Home is that I can log onto either one and I am *Using Facebook As* differently for each app. Sure, Facebook Home allows you to swap back and forth just as Facebook.com does on a computer, but by downloading and using the pages manager app, you no longer need to swap back and forth when on the go. If you want to check on your Fan page, simply open the pages manager app. Or if you want to check and see if you have received any likes on your most recent post or picture on your personal account, open the *Facebook Home*. It's that easy!

All three of these apps are available on the Apple App Store for iPhone, Google Play, Android Market, Windows Phone, and most other mobile platforms. Download them today and stay connected.

Mobile text integration

Many agencies are using text messages to market and promote homes. You can also use that technology to help build your following on Facebook as well. There is a fee associated with setting up a text messaging auto-responder account but it's well worth it. Over 95% of all text messages get opened within 5 minutes, that's a higher open rate than any other communications method... *by far*. As impressive as that is, we hear this comment all the time, "Well I would never want to get marketing messages via text." That's fine. Many other people do, as long as you are providing relevant information. Another comment we hear is, "I don't want to spam anyone." That is a valid point. You are not spamming anyone if they are asking you for information. You give them good content and the option to "opt-in" and "opt-out." If they get tired of your messages they can text STOP, just like an email unsubscribe button.

On your Fan page (along with your website and other social media sites), you can have an offer like this, "Text your name and email to 555-555-5555 for new listings." Another technique is to use a short code with a keyword. That type of campaign typically works like this "Text NEWHOMES to 58885 for the latest listings." (Not a live campaign.) John prefers to use name and email campaigns with a local number because you get their name, email and mobile number all at once.

You will not get as many people to sign up for text alerts when compared with an email campaign, however those that do are VERY hot leads. They are giving you their personal number to text them directly and permission to contact them. You can send automated replies that have links to video tours or pictures of your listings, pictures of homes on your Instagram account or any other creative thing you can think of. You can also follow up with email providing longer forms of content and information like free buyers or sellers guides, local sales data and more. There are systems available that integrate text, email, postcards, voicemails, DVD's, lead capture pages with video and more into an integrated campaign that will reach your prospects however they prefer.

This is a critical part of building your list. Any of the social media sites can delete your profile at any time and they do on occasion for a variety of reasons. If you have a bunch of Fans and your page gets suspended, how will you reach those people? You need to be continuously working to build your email, text message and snail

131

mail lists. Direct mail still works great, especially when you integrate social media, mobile offers and text messaging into your content. If you are working with buyers and sellers, you can build two lists, one for each demographic since the content you provide to each will be different.

QR Codes

QR codes (Quick Response Codes) have started gaining traction in the U.S. during the last few years and they are very popular in Asia and Europe. They are appearing regularly in mainstream ads nationally but they have not been wildly popular to date. We have included a QR code at the beginning and end of the book that takes you to our lead capture page where you can fill out your name and email to get bonus content. QR codes can also automatically open a smart phone's texting application and populate it with the phone number for the campaign.

There are multiple other uses they can be programmed for as well, like opening any of these: any web page, your fan page to get more likes, a free report in PDF format, a video, your Instagram pictures for a listing and surveys. Most of the sites to create QR codes will show you the options available with video tutorials so be creative. Best of all they are free and it takes little time to implement them. Be sure when you create them that they are at least 300 DPI (Dots per inch) to ensure they print clearly on larger formats. Some tools even allow you to upload an image or logo and build the code in color with the logo integrated so it will look nicer.

Including a QR code on a for sale sign, flyer, fan page, real estate magazine ad, direct mail piece, newspaper ad or TV ads is a compelling way for prospects to connect with your content quickly. You are taking them from the offline world to online without having to type domain names. The perception among people who use them will be that you are a tech savvy person and using all the tools at your disposal to market more effectively.

Insights, the Facebook analytics tool

How would you like to have the ability to learn and study all about your page's visitors? How about becoming informed of which posts people seem to engage with at a higher rate, and what doesn't quite make the mark? You can!

Facebook Insights allows you to analyze the ins and outs of your page. There are two ways to access this information: 1) On your Business page's *Admin Panel* in the bottom middle section you will find the *Insights* Dashboard. This is a snap shot of what is going on with your page in regards to perhaps the two most important pieces of data, *Reach* and *Talking About This*. 2) By clicking **See All** to the right of the section of the *Admin Panel* we just discussed. This will take you to a more in depth look at what is really going on.

Facebook's Insights has five subpages: *Overview, Likes, Reach, Talking About This*, and *Check-Ins. Likes, Reach* and *Talking about this* are opportunities to really break down your audience. Charts will be provided in each of these sections showing you the age and gender demographics as well as show you which are more active and in what quantities.

Overview- This tab provides you with a big picture snap shot including a chart representing all of your posts within the last 28 days. The graph at the top of the page is an amazing tool that shows you the *Total Likes, Friends of Fans, People Talking About This,* and *Weekly Total Reach* all in one place.

Likes- In this section of *Facebook Insights* you are allowed to change the date ranges in which the data will be displayed. You will be provided insights on people who like your page (demographics and location), broken down showing gender and age. As well as where your audience lives and what language they speak. Another tidbit of information you can find here is where your likes came from. For example your stats might look like: 32 On Page, 17 Mobile, 1 On Hover, 1 Friend Referrals.

Reach- How many people saw your posts? This is where you can take an in-depth look at who you are reaching, the quantity of unique users, and how many page views. These figures are so important and continuously striving to increase your reach should be at the forefront of your Facebook goals. Keep in mind that you can change the date range of the data displayed in the field provided in the top left corner under the *Overview* button.

Talking about this- How many engaged users do you currently have on your page? One thing that makes *Talking about this* so accurate is that the number displayed for this category is constantly changing and only represents the past 7 days. If today is May 10th, then the number of people *Talking about this* reflects the time period of 7 days ending yesterday. You will be looking at the stats for May 3rd through May 9th. Since this number is changing daily, it is the true testament to the success of your page.

Check-ins- Checking-in is a great way to share with your friends what you are up to and where you are going on Facebook. This is very popular among the younger crowd online and has been proven to be a very successful FREE marketing strategy for many businesses. *Check-ins* work very well for retail stores and restaurants as well as nightclubs and entertainment centers. This function of Facebook was not designed with real estate professionals in mind, but that doesn't mean that you can't benefit. If you regularly sit open houses or new construction model homes, this can be a tremendous tool creating awareness of your whereabouts and this might help increase traffic. Be sure that the address listed on your profile is the model home where you spend most of your workday. *Check-in* every day when you go to work, this will continuously increase your number of *Check-ins* on your page and will not show the world that it was you many times over and over again.

All of this data means nothing if you don't read it, understand it, and create a plan to improve upon it. I recommend that every month you sit down and look at your page's Insights and record the five posts that were the most engaging with the highest reach. To find these, click on **See All** to the right of the section of the *Admin Panel* called *Insights*. By default the overview tab will be selected and this is where you want to be. Scroll down past the plotted graph to the second section. Click on *Reach*, this will be the third column on the top of the chart. The results in the chart should now be in descending order from top to bottom organized by the total number of users reached. Notice that the number of engaged users should also follow the same descending order from top to bottom with few exceptions.

HINT: *If the numbers are in ascending order instead, click the Reach button once more and this should fix the problem.*

Now record the top five posts shown.

HINT: *Facebook Insights explains that figures are for the first 28 days after a post's publication only. What this means is that by default you are looking at a chart that represents a 28-day period. This is perfect for the exercise at hand, which analyzes one month at a time.*

For each post you've listed write down the answers to these questions:

- What type of post was it?

- What was the post about?

- How many people did this post reach?

- How many engaged users?

- How many users were Talking about this?

- What was the posts' virality percentage?

HINT: *Using a spread sheet or chart will make this much easier and organized.*

Now that you have recorded all of this data, let's dig in and find out what all of this really means! These are the five most successful posts for engaging your audience with the highest reach. Next, you must analyze the answers to the questions for each of the five posts.

- *What type of post was it?* How many of these posts were status updates? Shares? Photos or videos? Questionnaires or polls? If your answers cover the spread, you are doing great! But what if they were predominately status updates or photos? That's okay too! You are learning what is working so you can do more of it!

- *What was the post about?* Specifics are important, but for this exercise break the topics down into categories. Each person's categories might be slightly different and that's okay because each of your businesses is different. For example, imagine these were the topics you've come up with: Financing, local news or events, comic relief, food and dining, real estate specific, and market trends. Are your top five posts mostly categorized in the local events and news column? Or is the food and dining topic getting all the points? However the results turn out, look at the answers. Now you know which topics you've been posting about are getting the best responses. Focus on continuing to post about these topics and until next month's *Insights* evaluation.

- *How many people did this post reach?* The third column on the chart, under the *Overview* tab, is *Reach*. This is a very important figure; Facebook explains reach as *the number of unique people who have seen your post*. Obviously the more the better, but stop and think about this regarding the top five posts you've listed. What is it about these posts that made them reach the highest number of people? Did you share it on a few of your friend's timelines? Was the post asking a question or taking a poll that was really intriguing and interesting to your audience?

- *How many engaged users?* The fourth column on the chart is *Engaged Users*. This number is likely higher than the average post since you are analyzing only the cream of the crop. What is it about these five posts that were more engaging?

- *How many users were Talking about this? Talking about this* as I have mentioned before is the ultimate figure that can make or break your Business page. How does this actually work? Facebook explains this as *the number of unique people who have created a story from your post. Stories are created when someone likes, comments on or shares your posts; answers a question you posted; or responds to your event.* So this number is representing all of the interactions between your audience and the posts on your profile page.

- *What was the posts' virality percentage?* What is virality? *The percentage of people who have created a story from your post out of the total number of unique people who have seen it.* The goal is to achieve as high a virality percentage as possible, shoot for 25% virality on every post you create and continuously tweak your approach until you are able to maintain this number.

Pay Attention

Interact with your audience when they participate! You get a little red number on your mobile app every time someone posts or comments. Don't let it take over your day, but when you have a few minutes waiting in line somewhere, that is the perfect opportunity to reply. Thank them for contributing comments and likes then ask questions. This will draw them in even further into engagement and others will more likely see their conversation on your page and possibly jump in. See where this is going?

One trick I like do quite often is comment Using Facebook As my personal page on my Business page's posts. This way I can tag friends in my comments and this will bring more people into the conversation. Make sure you only tag people who are relevant to what you are posting about or who might find interest in your post; otherwise you may start to alienate people and annoy them.

Watch for negativity

Your business is your brand; protect it! Keep a close eye out for negative or derogatory comments or posts on your page. You have the option of deleting comments on your posts. This is easily done and it's an asset to any page administrator to ensure the protection of your page.

To delete a comment or post:

Step 1: Move your cursor over the comment or post that you wish to delete. An "X" should appear and you will see the word *Hide* if it is a comment you are deleting or the word *Remove* if it's something someone posted on your wall.

Step 2: Posts on your wall - Click the "X". If this was a post on your wall done by a third party you will find a drop down menu. These options will be available to you: *Default* (Allowed), *Highlighted on page, Allowed on page, Hidden from page, Delete,* or *Report/Mark as spam*. To delete, select delete. Feel free to click any of the other options if they are appropriate for the goal you are trying to accomplish.

Step 3: Comments on a post - Click the "X". You will find the comment is gone temporarily and you have some options to choose from. These are the selections that are available so just choose the appropriate action:

- Now this is only visible to the person who wrote it and their friends.
- Unhide
- Delete
- Report
- Ban (person)

Now you know how to protect your page from negativity and inappropriate posts so keep an eye out.

In Closing

Marketing on Facebook works really well if you set it up correctly and connect with people in your community. My team has experienced some incredible success in generating leads and revenue using Facebook. We were getting results in just a few weeks so it doesn't take that long to get started. To give you some more ideas, we added an extra chapter with links to a variety of Facebook Business pages that do a fantastic job of engaging their fans.

John and I want to thank you very much for investing your time to read our book. You have learned many of the tools and techniques needed to succeed in marketing your real estate business on Facebook and have a solid foundation to get started with. I spent a lot of time testing and tracking everything we taught in this book while building our lead generation pipeline. Now that it is up and running, it runs smoothly with a minimal amount of time and effort. You have the template to set up your business to get more leads and close more sales. Now Take Massive Action and get started! Oh, and if you please help us out and leave a review of this book at Amazon or wherever you bought it we would really appreciate it!

Our Bonus gift to you

To thank you for purchasing our book, you now have free access to our video training series "Top 5 Mistakes Real Estate Professionals Make on Facebook and How To Fix Them!" Just scan your receipt from Amazon then send it to the email below to get instant access to the bonus video training.

join-remarketingbook@instantcustomer.com

Need more help?

If you are still feeling a bit overwhelmed and need more help, we have a solution. You are busy; we understand how easy it is to get overwhelmed with information. You don't have the time to spend hours and hours trying to figure this out and then integrate it into your business. In just 15 to 20 minutes a week, you can stay on the cutting edge of social media tactics for your business and continuously improve your marketing to generate more leads. Our membership site offers weekly training videos where we discuss trends and teach you new techniques that are working in the real world. You can learn more about it here:

SocialMarketingTV.com

These video tutorials include step by step, on screen demonstrations from beginner to advanced of exactly how to set up your fan page, install apps and engage your users. We also feature success stories, Q&A sessions and interviews of industry leading agents, brokers and social media experts. Facebook and the rest of the social media sites are constantly changing. This is a fast and easy way for you to stay up to date on the latest changes and learn how to quickly implement them.

The videos are available for you to watch at your convenience and you can watch them on your mobile devices as well. It's an incredibly fast and inexpensive way to learn and implement the techniques you need to help you increase your revenue. Let's face it; if you are going to take the time to implement a strategy like this, a great return on investment is the only thing that matters. As a further benefit, once you get into the habit, it's a lot of fun! We hope you will take advantage of this opportunity and we look forward to seeing you inside the member's area.

Chapter 12

Great examples of engaging Business and Fan pages.

We searched far and wide to find other real estate professionals and companies that are doing well on Facebook. There are thousands that are doing a great job and I wanted to highlight a few. Take a moment and notice that these Business pages all have a few things in common: Posting constantly and consistently, relevant content for their communities, real estate statistics and reports, and highlighting their businesses. I found hundreds of pages with thousands of 'Likes' while searching, but what makes these stand out is the engagement they are getting, judged by their posts and the number *Talking About This*! That is the goal. Engagement and interaction from your audience is the key to generating leads and referrals. Remember, having a zillion 'Likes' doesn't matter as much as how many people are *Talking About This*. This indicates how many shares, likes and overall engagement you are getting on your page.

Real Estate Professionals

The Roman Lopez Real Estate Team
https://www.facebook.com/RomanLopezRealEstatePage

California Real Estate Information
https://www.facebook.com/CalifRealEstateInfo

Keller Williams Realty, Inc
https://www.facebook.com/KellerWilliamsRealty

Apartment Home Living
https://www.facebook.com/FindAFunPlace

Premier Real Estate
https://www.facebook.com/purplehomes

All Things Real Estate BHGRE
https://www.facebook.com/AllThingsRE

The Corcoran Group
https://www.facebook.com/thecorcorangroup

Non-Industry Related Fan Pages

This list has links to successful Fan pages that are non-industry related. The same thing applies here, how many people *Talking About This* is one of the most important metrics we measure. Learning to become successful often starts with studying those who have already experienced success.

Vin Diesel, The action actor has the largest Fan base on Facebook
https://www.facebook.com/VinDiesel

Coca-Cola
https://www.facebook.com/cocacola

The Cheesecake Factory
https://www.facebook.com/thecheesecakefactory

Publix
https://www.facebook.com/publix

NBC's "The Voice"
https://www.facebook.com/NBCTheVoice

Duke City Local
https://www.facebook.com/DukeCityLocal

The Chicken Chick
https://www.facebook.com/Egg.Carton.Labels.by.ADozenGirlz

Amazon.com
https://www.facebook.com/Amazon

Social Media Examiner - Top 10 Small Business Facebook Pages
http://www.socialmediaexaminer.com/top-10-
small-business-facebook-pages-2012-winners/

Harley Davidson
https://www.facebook.com/harley-davidson

###